Lincoln
AND
CHICAGO

Lincoln

AND

CHICAGO

JOHN TOMAN & MICHAEL FRUTIG

THE
History
PRESS

Published by The History Press
Charleston, SC
www.historypress.com

Cover image courtesy of the Robert R. McCormick Museum at Cantigny Park.

First published 2022

Manufactured in the United States

ISBN 9781467151665

Library of Congress Control Number: 2022935412

CONTENTS

Contents

ACKNOWLEDGEMENTS

My interest in Lincoln goes back to my childhood, and I have been researching materials for this book on and off for more than twenty-five years. I would like to acknowledge those individuals, friends and family, who encouraged me along the way. My great-aunt Ludina Aggen Mallory, who sparked my interest in Lincoln when I was a young boy. Mufti Mangan, my houseguest for many years, aided me in my research, compiling materials to form the extensive notes I used for this project. Pamela Pierrepont Bardo, a dear friend of mine who sits on the board of the Chicago Historical Museum, became interested in my numerous stories of Abraham Lincoln. I showed her my collection of pictures, books and articles on Lincoln and Chicago, and she helped organize material that had long sat on the shelf. She was amazed when she saw how much material I had collected and suggested that I write a book about Lincoln. Pamela found my writing partner, Michael Frutig, to assist me in creating this book, as I had a stroke that left me unable to do this endeavor alone. Mary Margaret Callaghan helped me start my book, and Louise Gram assisted in researching and editing materials. Christopher Phillips, who took a number of photographs for this book. Charlie Mowery, who helped with images and graphics. The Newberry Library's materials helped me research the people surrounding the Lincolns. The Chicago Historical Museum, where I gathered materials. The Library of Congress, where I found many of the pictures that brought the story to life. The Glessner House Museum and its curator William Tyre (glessnerhouse.org), whose collections and written works helped me understand life on Prairie Avenue. Father Lawler, who helped me piece together some of the threads of this story. Last but not at all least, I give a big thank you to my partner, Bill Bradt, for his years of companionship, care and patience, for his ever-present help in putting this together, especially his early help as I began this project. Without all this support, I could not have written this book, and for this I will be forever grateful.

—John Toman
May 2022

INTRODUCTION

It was during the Second World War, when I was just a boy, that I first came into contact with Abraham Lincoln. In Crawford School, now Corkery Elementary, in the office, there stood a bronze statue of President Lincoln, half life-size. It was a school that my entire family had attended. My grandmother, mother, aunts, uncles and I all went to that school at one time or another. During that war, the young teachers had been called away to serve their country, and my great-aunts came out of retirement to help fill the empty positions. You had to watch yourself in my aunt Mrs. Henpenius's classroom; she was very strict. Since a number of the teachers in the school were my relatives and friends, I spent a good deal of time in the office before and after school, with my aunt and the bronze Lincoln.

It was a striking statue, about my size at the time: his protruding nose and pointed chin, the wizened eyes and a humble smile on his lips. Here was a troubled man with an enormous burden to bear. Through all my years of schooling, through classes on American history, the statue in my grade school stands out as my most vivid memory of Lincoln.

When I was a boy, my aunts would often take me to museums to satisfy my interest in history and antiques, or else to the fantastically elegant Marshall Fields, where I spent hours looking at the marvelous colonial antiques and beautiful silver. I often went with my grandmother and her sisters to the Lawndale-Crawford Historical Society, of which I would later be president, to attend the meetings and lectures. I listened to it all eagerly. Occasionally, if I was lucky, I could sit in on meetings of the Ninety-Three'ers. This was originally just a social club for those who had worked at the magnificent Columbian Exhibition of 1893, but as membership dwindled with time, it began to include people who had attended the fair. My grandmother had gone to the fair as a child and was a member. They used to meet just off of Prairie Avenue, on Twenty-First Street.

I went with my grandmother when the Ninety-Three'ers were celebrating the anniversary of the World's Fair in Chicago. There was a reception and a picnic in Jackson Park where the fair had been held. I met Little Egypt, a dancer at the fair who had enthralled audiences from around the world with her hootchie-kootchie dance (a risqué belly dance); by the time I met her, she was a sweet little old lady. Later, I met a 107-year-old man who had been a guard at the fair. This man asked me if I wanted to shake the hand of a man who shook the hand of Abraham Lincoln. I took him up on his offer. I was now one handshake away from the man behind that statue.

My interest in Lincoln was kindled, but it took time for that to grow. In junior high school, I was chosen by my teachers (for being an outstanding student) to go down to Springfield for a mock gubernatorial election, an annual event called Boys State. When we weren't at the fairgrounds participating in the event, we were taken to see all the Lincoln spots in and around the city. The old capitol building where he worked, his home and neighborhood—we even went to New Salem where he lived and worked after moving away from his parents. We also visited the elegant new capitol building. All of this combined with my previous experience with Lincoln into a powerful portrait of the man.

Years later, I acquired a scrapbook of memorabilia, filled with telegrams and printed material from before the Great Chicago Fire; it was rare to have so much paper from before that calamity. In it, I discovered a number of newspaper clippings of life in Chicago, with some mention of the Lincoln family. One of the pieces was a telegram sent as the fire raged, inquiring whether the lumberyards were in danger. They were. This piece I gave to the Chicago Historical Society.

All my life, I have worked as a florist, and through that work I came twice to meet the last of the Lincoln line, Robert Lincoln Beckwith, grandson of Robert Lincoln and great-grandson of Abraham Lincoln. The first time was in the seventies, while working for a Michigan Avenue flower shop. I was decorating the Playboy Mansion in Chicago for Christmas. In the ballroom, we set up a twenty-two-foot Christmas tree, and as I was decorating it, Hugh Hefner and an elderly gentleman came in. This gentleman was short, stocky, shy—but when he started talking, a congenial man. This was Robert

Lincoln Beckwith, and he told Hefner and me how the house had belonged to Dr. George Snow Isham, a friend of Robert's, and how each Christmas they would come to that house and a sleigh would be set in the ballroom beside the tree, overflowing with presents. Christmas was a fun time for the Lincolns in Chicago.

The second time came nearly a decade later. I was hired to do the flowers for a party at a home in Lake Forest, Illinois. It sat right along the shores of Lake Michigan. As I brought in flowers, I saw Robert Beckwith again and greeted him. After a brief conversation, I went to help decorate the garden. At this point, I had been fascinated with the Lincolns for some time and had begun to acquire Lincoln paraphernalia, including a chair from his law practice in Springfield and one from the home of the Gourleys, his neighbors.

The chairs came to me in a strange way. A patron of my flower shop, who would stop by to talk from time to time, had her family home in Springfield. She moved some of the furniture to Chicago after her place was burglarized, old furniture piled up in her Cadillac for the drive. She knew my interest in history and invited me to come see her collection, telling me all about each piece. When she passed, her children offered me anything I wanted from her home. She had told me the history of the chairs, which she inherited from her mother. I took them without hesitation.

A late piece of the puzzle came in the early 2000s, when I was sitting outside my cardiac rehab clinic. I was waiting for the valet to bring my car around and got to talking to the man sitting next to me. It turned out that he was Leonard Sauer, owner of one of my favorite restaurants. He told me the story of his place, how it was built to be a ballroom for Prairie Avenue debutants and a dance studio. After the neighborhood declined, it had the top floors removed and was converted to a warehouse. He acquired it and turned the open space into a German restaurant. After closing, the entire kitchen would be cleaned and leftover food given to the needy. I told him I used to go to that restaurant regularly with friends; the food was delicious, and the service was perfect.

John Toman's chair, which he was told came from the Lincoln office. *Collection of John Toman.*

The drawing is from *Frank Leslie's Illustrated Newspaper* vol. 11, showing the Lincoln office. John Toman's chair is second from the right. *Abraham Lincoln Presidential Library and Museum.*

Sauer told me that of course his waiters were the best: they were all former Pullman staff, trained to be perfect gentlemen. The first men Pullman hired were former house slaves. When the Pullman Palace Car Company was made to shut down, Sauer had hired them; after all, they were world famous for their service. By this time, I had learned that Robert Todd Lincoln had been president of Pullman, another connection.

I am also a junker; going about antique shops, if there was a book on Lincoln or Chicago, I bought it. I had begun gathering many stories about the Lincolns and the people around them, some that were squirreled away and overlooked. One particular aspect of Lincoln that puzzled me was his speech. It seemed older than the time he lived in, epic in size, vivid and commanding in style. Through all my research, I could not find an answer to this curiosity of mine until I read Joe Wheeler's *Abraham Lincoln, a Man of Faith and Courage.* In this excellent book, I learned that a young Abraham read from the King James Bible (one of the few books available to people on the frontier) when he was finished with his chores or at Sunday school. The reason, then, that Abraham's speech is so biblical is because he copied the style deliberately, influenced by the Bible from a very early age.

As a dyslexic, I have to read material a couple of times in order to understand it. By the time I do, I have it memorized. As I read, looking for the story I wanted to tell, I kept finding new aspects of history that brought the stories to life. All this material was stuck in my mind, waiting to get out, the story growing and growing until a little pamphlet became a full book. As the collection of Lincoln artifacts and stories grew, my mind was resolved to put it together.

But so much has been written about Lincoln, a vast number of books analyzing his every presidential moment from all sides—or else the story of the humble prairie lawyer, going the circuit from county to county to earn his family bread. Yet I had all this material and knowledge about Lincoln in between these periods of his life, about his time in my hometown, and so little was written about it.

The Lincolns were tied inextricably to the city of Chicago, before and after the presidency of their patriarch. In all the years of Abraham's life, he came to the city numerous times. His work for railroad companies and industrial moguls brought him to the city quite often. Chicago is where he would give many of his famous speeches. It is where he met the owners of the *Chicago Tribune*, the newspaper that would ceaselessly work to make him president, using every trick in the book to secure his nomination. Chicago saw the first Lincoln-Douglas debate, and it is where Lincoln would plan his elections with Norman B. Judd, the Chicagoan who offered the city for the Republican Convention of 1860 specifically so that Lincoln would have a home field advantage. Chicago loved Abraham so much, he had to hide himself in order to get work done or else be mobbed by demands to make speeches.

Chicago was a miracle city in Lincoln's time. Incorporated in 1837, Chicago began as a fur-trading town huddled close to Fort Dearborn. On the edge of the expanding nation, the city was well situated beside the lake and the river. By 1850, it was full of railroads, a transportation hub connecting the interior to the coastal ports. All railroads led to Chicago. It had grown with immigrants and entrepreneurs, full of factories that spewed forth the machines of the Second Industrial Revolution. Twenty years from hovels to industrial powerhouse, transportation hub and the crown jewel of the West. By the time of the Civil War, Chicago was a model Northern city, with booming docks and busy train stations. Its people read major metropolitan newspapers, watched fine theater and opera, debated the future of slavery and hosted elegant parties.

My grandmother told me that when she was young, there was one Democrat in the entire Crawford community. The Republican Party was founded in 1854 by former Whigs in Ripon, Wisconsin, as a party aimed at stopping the further expansion of slavery. They were a diverse lot, with abolitionists and big business interests, Free-Soil Party members and capitalists. Chicago, by the time of the founding of the party, was a booming city, quickly becoming a

Republican bastion. Republican Chicago had a strong pull on Abraham. The *Chicago Tribune* was a major Republican paper, a vocal voice on the Kansas-Nebraska Act and the growing divide between North and South.

A divide between the mercantile North and cash-crop South can be seen clearly from the very foundation of the United States, only growing in the following years. The two different systems relied on one another but were diametrically opposed to each other. It was the North that fed the United States. The cash crops of tobacco, indigo and, more than any other, cotton are thirsty crops that destroy the fertility of the soil. Cash crops, and therefore slavery, had need for expansion, and there was plenty of money and power backing these interests. When the war started, the South discovered that they had created vast systems for cash crops but not food.

Immigrants from all over Europe poured across the Atlantic in the years after 1848, the great year of revolution. They had fought for the right to a constitution and lost; fleeing retribution, they came to the New World. Upon their arrival, they found good land to farm, whereas Europe had too little to feed all its people. German, Irish, French, Italian, Polish and Jewish, they all came for the individual liberty they were denied in Europe. These people soon found themselves embroiled in a war for their adopted home, one they fought with zeal.

Immigrant populations came to the northwestern states and fueled their activity. There was no work in the South that a laborer would be hired for. Slaves were the engine of the South, and immigrant labor was neither needed nor wanted, but the North had room to spare for them and welcomed them with open arms. Factories and farms ran on their labor. The northwestern states at the time—Illinois, Michigan, Indiana, Wisconsin, Iowa and Minnesota—were where the United States got its food. Lumber and wheat, lead and steel: all the things a growing nation needed were right there in that one corner. The food, machines and all kinds of manufactured goods spewed out of the Midwest to consumers. The region was full of waterways for transport, huge swamps stretching throughout the Chicagoland area and into Indiana (the swamps were so full of birds that they became known as the Butcher Shop of Chicago). It was easy to get from place to place by water, and when the railroads came in, it became that much easier to move all the bountiful resources to where they were needed. The Midwest fed and still feeds the United States and the world. It was the right place at the right time, and Chicago was at the heart of it all. The city was vital to the Union effort, not least because it had molded the man in the White House.

Why is it that the place where Lincoln met his richest, most influential backers is left out of the story? Why are the tricks they pulled to get Lincoln nominated not included in biographies? There are so many fantastic small pieces to the story of Abraham and his family, and as I was compiling my notes, there always seemed to be something more to add, something new to tell. The history of all the people who banded together to make Abraham Lincoln the president, at times against his will, has faded in the shadow of the war he was forced to fight.

All the characters from the Lincolns' age are gone now, most traces of their lifestyle have disappeared and all that is left is hidden between the pages of books. It can be found, but only if one takes the time to look. I have been looking, for decades, at the small details from 150 years ago, tucked away in this or that history book. The intense love that so many Chicagoans had for Abraham Lincoln and their desire to see him president deserves to be told. Their stories and their influence on him are an important piece of the puzzle. It is in order to tell these stories that I put this book together.

Chapter 1

THE ROAD TO CHICAGO

The United States was going west, past the Appalachians and into the wild prairies beyond. The country was newly independent, with borders stretching to the Mississippi, and pioneers were eager to stake a claim on untouched land. The people who had come to the Thirteen Colonies were willing to risk their lives in the dangerous Atlantic crossing for a chance at a better life. Life in the New World was harsh, but they kept coming. In England, they were the poor, the maligned, the marginalized, but all were adventurous. They passed down their daring spirit, so when independence was won, Americans were packing their bags. In the Old World, land was owned by aristocracy going back a thousand years, and no one could get their own piece. But in the United States, it was practically endless. A pioneer could lay claim to any land he came across, so long as no one was there first. This could be a dangerous position, as they would be miles from civilization and all its protection. The native Indian tribes were by no means willing to surrender their land to the slowly encroaching United States. Fierce skirmishes happened with regularity, as both the pioneers and Indians fought for their right to the land. It was a chaotic running battle, but one in which the pioneers had the upper hand. As they pushed, their nation followed them; pioneer towns where anything was possible sprung up. It was on the shores of Lake Michigan that the son of pioneers and a pioneer town would meet and together shape their nation.

The first non-natives in the region were French. Explorers and fur traders, they pushed deep into the continent to find new lands for their king, their

God and their wallets. Hoping to map the upper Mississippi and perhaps discover where it met the sea, Father Jacques Marquette and Louis Joliet set out from French outposts in Wisconsin in 1673. A Jesuit priest, Marquette was assigned to minister to the Ottawa tribes in what is today the Upper Peninsula of Michigan. He left Quebec in 1668 and established various missions throughout the Great Lakes region. Louis Joliet was born in the New World in 1645 and was training to be a priest when the allure of life as a fur trapper and explorer caused him to leave the settled colony of New France for the wild interior. For five years, he travelled through the Great Lakes as a private fur trader, before he was given instructions to join Father Marquette on an expedition, "marking down the rivers on which we were to sail, the names of the nations and places through which we were to pass, the course of the great river, and what direction we should take when we got to it." In the courts of Europe, France had laid claim to the entire Great Lakes region and was eager to chart the new dominion. The two men left from the mission of St. Ignace on May 17, 1673.

Marquette and Joliet traveled down Lake Michigan and portaged across various rivers to reach the Mississippi. They mapped their way as far as the Arkansas River, turning back for fear of hostile tribes and Spaniards. On the return, they were told by the friendly Illinois tribes that the Illinois River was much easier to row up than the Wisconsin and that at the river's end, there was an easy, swampy portage to the Che-cau-gou River and from there to Lake Michigan and French territory. The name Che-cau-gou is of uncertain origin. In the language of the Illinois, it meant "great" or "powerful," but in the language of the Chippewa it referred to skunk or wild onions. As they traveled up the south branch of the river, the explorers made special note of the portage as an excellent location for a canal. While Marquette and Joliet were the first to map the area, French fur traders had used the portage for years.

The years following the expedition saw an increase in French activity around the Chicago portage, which became a thoroughfare for fur traders. French settlers lived farther west, such as in St. Louis and on the eastern shore of the Mississippi, but not in Chicago. Fur traders erected a number of temporary buildings but would move with the seasons. Joliet told the authorities of New France that a canal could connect the Mississippi to the

Opposite: Fur traders were the first Europeans in much of North America. While the coast was heavily populated by colonists, the inland was explored by few, mainly traders and priests. *Frederick Remington. Courtesy of the Tennessee State Library & Archives.*

Above: The Potawatomi were the Indigenous people of the Chicago area and had close ties to the French. *Library of Congress LC-DIG-cwpbh-01557.*

Great Lakes. Explorer René-Robert Cavelier, Sieur de La Salle, was less sure. Travelling across the portage many times during the 1680s, he wrote to his superiors that such a project was unfeasible, and when Joliet died, the project was forgotten. Relations between France and native Indians were for the most part friendly, as only fur traders came to the region, and their interactions were beneficial to both. The Catholic church did send a mission to the Chicago area (the exact location is disputed), but it failed within a couple years. France would lose control of the region in the Seven Years' War, at which point it was transferred to Great Britain, whose relations with the tribes in the area were more strained.

Jean Baptist Point Du Sable was the first permanent non-Indigenous resident of the Chicago River area. He was a free Black man and is thought to have come from Hispaniola. He settled near the mouth of the Chicago River. The first mention of his small cabin comes from the journal of the British commander of Michilimackinac, Colonel Arent DePeyster, in 1779. He wrote, "Baptiste Point DeSailble, a handsome negro, well-educated and settled in Eschikagou; but much in the French interest." In 1788, Du Sable married a Potawatomi woman named Kitihawa in Cahokia on the Mississippi, in both Potawatomi and Catholic ceremonies. Thanks to his good relations with the Potawatomi of the region, his trading post was successful; soon, Du Sable had a mill, a smokehouse, a workshop, a barn and stable and a dairy with thirty head of cattle. Following American victory, Britain ceded all land east of the Mississippi to the United States. The new nation originally had little interest in the region and had a "live and let live" policy concerning the Indian tribes there. The new territory was far from population centers, and settlers were more interested in Ohio and Kentucky. Du Sable got a land grant from the United States in 1783, the first such grant to be given in the Chicago area. The only major legislation affecting the area was the Northwest Ordinance, which banned slavery in the territory.

As time went on and Kentucky and Tennessee became fully settled states, Americans began to pay more attention to the northwest. The first sign of change came in 1803, when Fort Dearborn was built at the mouth of the Chicago River. It aimed to protect the fur traders, but it was chronically undermanned and not a top priority. In 1809, John Jacob Astor formed the American Fur Company, chartered in New York, to compete against British fur traders. The American Fur Company operated around the Chicago River and saw large returns, making Astor a millionaire, the first to become rich from the Chicago area. Around this time, Du Sable left to pursue an opportunity in Missouri, but four families had moved into the area near the fort: those of Ouilmette, Burns, Lee and Kinzie. Kinzie bought Du Sable's home and store. All four men were traders and farmers who enjoyed close ties to the nearby tribes. These were the beginnings of Chicago.

Soon after, however, Chicago was almost erased from the map. When the War of 1812 began, most western Indian tribes sided with the British, as they had become increasingly frustrated with the way the Americans treated them. In the Chicago area, the Potawatomi joined the British. The position of Fort Dearborn was untenable, and an evacuation was planned. They offered to give whiskey and ammo to the Potawatomi in return for safe passage, but the night before leaving, the commander of the fort changed his mind and had all these goods destroyed. A caravan of soldiers and their families evacuated the fort, walking the lakeshore toward Fort Wayne in Indiana, a few friendly native guides at their side. Word spread that the garrison had gone back on the deal, and the enraged Potawatomi hid in the dunes. Once the column was well out of reach of the fort, the Potawatomi attacked, and of the 148 people who left the fort, 86 were killed in the ambush. There were many notable instances of natives on both sides trying to protect the women and children present at the massacre, yet they were mostly unsuccessful. The day after the massacre, the Potawatomi razed the fort to the ground. The location of the battle is uncertain, but it probably took place between Calumet Street and Prairie Avenue on Eighteenth Street. The only resident to stay afterwards was Ouilmette, who had married a Potawatomi woman and was safe from violence.

After the war, the United States dealt harshly with those tribes that sided with the British, forcing the sale of their land, including the land around the Chicago River, and removing them across the Mississippi. The federal government owned much of the land in the territories and sold it to private landowners, expressly forbidding Indian tribes from selling to individuals. A second, better prepared Fort Dearborn was built on the foundations of the old. One of the first to return to Chicago was Jean Baptiste Beaubien, a Frenchman born in Detroit. He had purchased a home in the Chicago area in 1812 after the massacre, most likely the home of Lee. He returned when the army did.

With the natives removed, the Illinois territory began preparing for statehood. The territorial delegate for Illinois, Nathaniel Pope, brought forward a bill to reshape its boundaries. The original charter for the territory placed its northernmost border tangent with the southern tip of Lake Michigan, such that the state had no lakefront. Pope pointed to the success of Indiana's redrawn borders, granting it a lakefront and allowing the construction of ports. His bill gave Illinois ten miles of lakefront in order to boost the state's economy, connecting it to financial centers such as New York and Pennsylvania. While the bill was in committee, he proposed a further increase to the 42°30' latitude, adding 8,500 square miles and 41 additional miles of lakefront. This new line included Chicago. Pope saw the site as an excellent location for a port and pointed out that the Chicago Portage would eventually be made into a canal and the canal being split between two states was unfeasible. His argument that a port could connect the resources of Illinois to the east coast as well as to the Mississippi was well received, and Congress approved the new borders. Pope's efforts created the modern borders of the state, adding many prosperous communities, such as Galena and its lead mines. Even before it was a town, the fortunes of Chicago were tied to the proposed canal that would connect the Great Lakes to the Gulf of Mexico. Illinois joined the Union in 1818 as the twenty-first state.

Around the same time that Chicago was beginning, far across the prairies, in a Kentucky log cabin, Thomas Lincoln and Nancy Hanks were expecting a child. Their home had only a single room and a single window; the door hung on leather hinges, and the floor was dirt that had been patted down. Nancy lay in labor on the bed of cornhusks and bearskins, Thomas and the midwife helping as they could. Shortly after dawn on February 12, 1809, the wailing of a newborn babe filled the still winter morning. The boy was named after his grandfather; the infant Abraham Lincoln rested in his mother's arms, warmed by a fire and the bearskins. As an adult, he spoke little of his ancestry, writing in his campaign autobiography that it was nothing unheard of in "the short and simple annals of the poor." This was not entirely true, as his father's side owned quite a bit of property, and his mother's side were middle-class folks. Both families had come from Virginia to stake out a claim in Kentucky, the pioneer spirit driving them there.

Abraham's father's family had been in the New World for some time, with records of a Puritan Samuel Lincoln, a respected weaver, landing in the Massachusetts Bay Colony in 1637. Samuel arrived in the colonies eighteen years after the first African slaves were brought and seventeen after the *Mayflower* landed at Plymouth. His descendants would later move to Pennsylvania and become Quakers; then, a generation later, some went on to settle in Virginia. There, the fourth generation of the Lincoln family had a nice home and a number of slaves. One of their sons, looking to make his own legacy, moved west in search of land. This was Abraham's grandfather, also named Abraham, and he acquired about 5,000 acres of farmland in Kentucky. A captain in the Revolutionary War, this Abraham moved his young family across the Appalachians into the Blue Grass. He was followed into Kentucky by his brother, who settled in a much more fertile area and quickly became a wealthy man and slave owner. Abraham was shot suddenly by Indians while he was planting corn. His eight-year-old son Thomas saw this and ran to hold his dead father just as the assailant emerged from the woods, moving quickly toward Thomas. A second shot rang out suddenly, and the attacker fell—Thomas's brother Mordecai had shot the Indian and saved Thomas's life. This was a story that played out frequently on the fringes of the new nation. Orphaned and the youngest of three brothers, Thomas got none of his father's estate and had to fend for himself when he came of age.

Thomas Lincoln, now without any means of support, took to wandering and working odd jobs throughout the Kentucky territory, settling on a career as a carpenter. He had to scrape by, day by day, living hand to mouth from an early age. An additional barrier to success was his illiteracy, making him the black sheep of a well-off landed family. He had no interest in learning to read and didn't find the skill practical. Despite this, he had some renown as a storyteller, a skill that his son would learn on his knee. Slowly, Thomas was able to build an estate and home, so that by the time of Abraham's birth he had a modest amount of property, about one hundred acres of land. In addition to carpentry, he bought and leased land around Elizabethtown, Kentucky.

The story of Abraham's mother is murky, but there is evidence to suggest that she was an illegitimate child. His grandmother, Lucy Hanks, had been brought up on charges of fornication, and the daughters of the Hanks family had a number of other illegitimate children. Abraham would be close to his Hanks cousins all his life. Nancy married Thomas Lincoln in 1806. She was literate and would teach the young Abraham his letters, encouraging him to read, something that would capture his interest far more than the farm labor required of him.

The world Abraham was born into was one on the cusp of great change. Since the dawn of civilization, the vast majority of people had worked in agriculture and the fastest methods of travel were by horse and sail. Small improvements were always being made, but the human race had never seen the pace of innovation that came with the Industrial Revolution. The cotton gin, reaper and steel plow were all innovations that would change how many hands were needed for farm work, and the unneeded labor went to cities. Steam power, first implemented in textiles, was soon made into the steam engine, and the world was forever changed. First used in boats, the steam engine allowed for travel against the wind. At the time of Abraham's birth, steamboats already travelled up and down the Mississippi. Improvements to steam power continued through the nineteenth century, and the world that saw the century's end was unrecognizable from the one that saw its beginning. Additionally, America's involvement in the transatlantic slave trade ended in 1807, though slavery persisted on increasingly large plantations; slave labor supplied the raw goods that northern factories turned into manufactured goods.

When Abraham was two, the family moved to Knob Creek, Kentucky, the first home he remembered. Because Thomas owned and rented land, he was often embroiled in lawsuits. Kentucky's laws of land ownership left plenty to be desired, and others claimed the land Thomas had deeds to. He lost each suit and lost large tracts of land and the rents that came from them. These protracted court battles perhaps later became motivation for Abraham to learn law. A frustrated Thomas Lincoln would move his family to Indiana in 1816, where the property laws were stronger.

Abraham's parents attended the Little Pigeon Baptist Church, which opposed slavery, alcohol and dancing. His father was involved with its functions, becoming an elder of the church. Thomas hated slavery and was temperate, traits that were passed to Abraham despite their contentious relationship. As he grew, Abraham came to dislike organized religion, but he was not irreligious, as later claimed. Even as late as 1860, only 23 percent of Americans attended church weekly.

Abraham had an older sister, Sarah Lincoln, as well as a younger brother who died only a few days after his birth. Sarah would walk Abraham to school, and when they weren't helping their father, they were together. When tragedy came, they had only each other to lean on. In 1818, Nancy fell ill from milk sickness (a disease caused by drinking milk from a cow that had eaten white snakeroot) and died. Abraham was nine. This first great loss of his life was devastating to him, and it was a long time before he stopped grieving. Sarah was charged with the household, cooking and cleaning for Thomas, Abraham and their cousin Dennis Hanks. Dennis was the orphaned cousin of Abraham's mother, and though there was a ten-year difference between him and Abraham, the pair were fast friends. Dennis helped out on the farm, as did another Hanks cousin, John, who lived nearby. When finished with his farm work, Abraham would read aloud by the fireside, keeping his sister company. A year after the death of his wife, Thomas would remarry Sarah Bush Johnston, also a widower with children.

A painting of the Lincoln home at Knob Creek, Kentucky, where Abraham grew up between the ages of two and eight. Returning to the place years later, Lincoln wrote a poem that began: "My childhood home I see again, / And sadden with the view; / And still, as memory crowds my brain, / There's pleasure in it too…" *Collection of John Toman.*

Sarah was a kind stepmother to her new children; she treated them as her own and made sure they received an education, being educated herself. Sarah encouraged Abraham to read, and he would borrow books from neighbors, reading whatever he could get his hands on: biographies of George Washington and Benjamin Franklin, as well as books on mathematics and rhetoric. *Robinson Crusoe* was a favorite. The only book his illiterate father owned was the King James Bible, whose stories the boy would memorize and whose distinct lyrical cadence became part of his speech. Abraham got along well with his new mother; the two of them shared a sense of humor. Once, Sarah told him to wash his hair so as to not leave marks on the ceiling, and as a joke, Abraham picked up his stepbrother and had him leave muddy footprints on the ceiling. Sarah laughed when she found them, admonishing him to clean it up.

Thomas Lincoln has received a reputation through the years of being a harsh disciplinarian, always punishing Abraham. In truth, he had a family to feed and needed all the help he could get, especially as his eyesight failed. In his recollections, Abraham made his father out to be a rough man, but

Above: Painting of Abraham Lincoln splitting rails as a teenager, working for his father. The wood was used for shingles, boards, furniture, fence posts and firewood. When running for the Republican nomination and for president, the Rail-Splitter image helped portray him as an honest worker. *Collection of John Toman.*

Left: *The Young Lincoln* by Charles Keck, c. 1945. Created for the Grand Army of the Republic, the statue now stands at Senn Park in Chicago, a testament to the legend of Abraham's youth still told today. Though he disliked his rough childhood, it was a boon to his political fortunes later in life. *Christopher Phillips.*

if Abraham had his way, he would have been reading all day. Abraham, while tall and strong, cared more about books than farm work, but as a boy, there was little his book learning could do to help the household, while his manual labor could contribute to their financial situation. Abraham was not unskilled when it came to physical labor—he was handy with an axe and had split several thousand rails with his cousin John Hanks—but his mind was always focused on what new things could be gained from reading, frequently ignoring his chores to read a book. In those days, it was common for the money earned by a child to go to the head of the household. Thomas was a man who had to work for every penny, illiterate and rugged, who had lost everything in his childhood and was evicted from a number of homesteads, always forced to rebuild; he needed all the help he could get. In this simple lifestyle, Abraham grew from a boy to a young man: tall, lanky, but powerfully built.

A wealthy merchant by the name of James Gentry was sending his son down to New Orleans with goods to sell. Abraham, at the age of nineteen and with some experience rafting, served as a deckhand and went down the Mississippi. It was in New Orleans that Abraham first saw a slave market and slavery in its cruelest form, the sight of which shocked him. Having grown up in Kentucky, he had seen some slaves, but never before had he been confronted with the sheer brutality of slavery. He was eager to return to the free soil of Indiana. Upon his return, Abraham gave his earnings to his father.

Shortly after Abraham's return, his sister died in childbirth, a devastating blow as she was his closest friend. According to Abraham, depression was common in the Lincoln family; Abraham's uncle Mordecai and his children were prone to bouts of it. Abraham, too, seems to have had it, brought on by the losses of his early life. At the recommendation of John Hanks, Thomas moved his family into Illinois, the frontier at the time, settling in Macon County, near Springfield. There, he and Abraham built a new home, and Abraham continued working odd jobs to help out.

Not too far away from the new Lincoln homestead, Chicago became a town. Beaubien would become an agent of the American Fur Company and thrived among the few families who lived around the rebuilt fort. By 1825, he was the wealthiest man in Chicago, with a thousand dollars to his name. His brother Mark came to the settlement in 1826. Mark established the Sauganash Hotel, Chicago's first, which quickly became famous in the sparse territory for its bar, dancing and the proprietor's skill with the violin. Congress and various state legislatures had tried numerous times to build a canal, but these plans fell apart before a single shovel hit the dirt. In 1829, the state legislature was ready to try again to connect Michigan and the Mississippi, creating a commission to "locate the canal, to lay out towns, to sell lots, and apply the proceeds to the construction of the canal." Members of the commission and Chicago's city fathers were Dr. Jayne of Springfield, Edmund Roberts of Kaskaskia and Charles Dunn. They hired James Thompson to survey and plat the towns. He surveyed Chicago and designated it Section 9, Township 39, Range 14. Its population was around one hundred, half of which was Catholic. Chicago soon became the county seat of Cook County and received a population boom, doubling in size by 1833. Cook County was named for Daniel Cook, a congressman and rising star in Illinois politics, who died young. He had been married to Julia Edwards, daughter of Ninian Edwards, who was governor when Illinois was still a territory. As Illinois became a state, Cook defeated a push to introduce slavery into the state by powerful landed interests. The last of the native Potawatomi left in 1835 after signing a deal with the government and began their long trek across the Mississippi to a reservation in Missouri. Five thousand came to Chicago for the last of their annuities, and as they left, eight hundred braves led the procession with their war dance, passing beneath the windows of the Sauganash Hotel as they left what had been their home.

In 1831, John Hanks and Abraham, as well as Abraham's stepbrother John Johnston, set out by canoe on the Sangamon River to Springfield. They were on their way to see Denton Offutt, who needed them to take a shipment to New Orleans. This trip proved to be a deciding moment in Abraham's life, as the journey would be hazardous. Their boat ran aground several times and Abraham, facing challenges, had to come up with solutions on the fly. When trapped on a milldam at New Salem, Abraham figured out a way to free the raft by lifting one side and drilling a hole to drain water. The experience served to demonstrate his cleverness, as well as his understanding of mechanical principles, impressive for a largely self-taught man. This memory would serve to drive Lincoln's own invention, which would come many years later, and spark his interest in making the waterways more navigable. It was on this journey that he gained the confidence to become his own man. He would not return to work for his father; at twenty-two, he was ready to move on.

Upon returning from New Orleans, Abraham did not go home to Macon County but instead went to live in New Salem, the town where he had been stranded on the milldam. He was given a job in Offutt's general store. Almost immediately after his arrival, Lincoln ran for the Illinois State Legislature and lost. It was the only general election defeat of his life. He would not have much time to process this defeat, as the Blackhawk War broke out on April 6, 1832.

The war had been building for decades. In 1804, the United States took large portions of Sauk land in the Treaty of St. Louis. Blackhawk, a Sauk chief who deeply resented the loss of land, went west of the Mississippi and fought alongside the British in the War of 1812. In the late 1820s, the United States began to survey the land taken in the Treaty of St. Louis and parcel it out to white settlers, further enraging Blackhawk. Because of his opposition to the United States, Blackhawk had come to lead a small band of Indians who had abandoned their various tribes to join him. This group was named the British Band because they flew the Union Jack as a symbol of their resistance. They crossed the Mississippi with five hundred warriors and six hundred noncombatants.

In response to the threat, the United States organized a militia of six thousand men with approximately five hundred regular army troops and a small additional number of allied Indians. When he heard of the war, Lincoln volunteered immediately. He was elected captain of the militia from New Salem, later saying of this honor, "Not since had any success in life gave so much satisfaction." Abraham spent the war far from the battles, though he did take part in the burning of Prophet's Town, an Indian village, and helped dig graves for the dead at Stillman's Run. He spent most of the war marching up and down the Rock River area. His gentle spirit held his militia in check, preventing his company from attacking unarmed Indians. He later described his time in the war, saying, "I had many bloody battles with musquetoes [*sic*]." According to various accounts given long after the fact, Abraham came as far north as Wisconsin during the war, but there is no substantial evidence to support this. The war was short-lived, ending on August 27 the same year. Abraham did not see combat, but the war would have a profound impact on his life.

This was the first time Lincoln was in a social setting with educated people, and many of them would become lifelong friends and patrons, including perhaps the most consequential person of his life, his benefactor John T. Stuart. Handsome and tall, Stuart was from the well-bred Kentucky gentry. He was one of the few regular army officers in the conflict, a major in the battalion Lincoln served in. Lincoln was a store clerk, but Stuart, impressed by his intelligence and charm, saw great potential. He and Lincoln were soon fast friends, and after the war, Stuart pressed Lincoln to put his mind to work as a lawyer. He was a lawyer himself, having passed the bar in 1828, and offered to take Lincoln on as a junior partner. With the ever-present support of Stuart, Lincoln began studying law. Stuart even lent him his law books. The war also introduced Lincoln to John Calhoun, who would give him a leg up in a short time.

When the war ended, Lincoln returned to New Salem and Offutt's store and worked as postmaster, miller, store clerk and bartender. He would spend much of his time in the smithy of Joshua Miller and was considering becoming a blacksmith for a time, but a reading of Blackstone's *Commentaries* kept his focus on becoming Stuart's partner. Lincoln kept up with the news by reading the papers he delivered, often delivering mail to homes miles away, though it was not required of him. Abraham was now in the center of life in New Salem and came to know the people of the area. They, in turn, came to admire the tall outsider as a fixture of their small town. Occasionally, he would wrestle locals in good-natured contests behind the general store.

In 1833, Lincoln was given the job of deputy county surveyor by John Calhoun, who was, at that time, the Sangamon County surveyor. Pollard Simmons, a resident of New Salem, suggested Lincoln to Calhoun. Lincoln's interest in surveying may have gone back to his childhood, when he read a biography of George Washington, who had been a surveyor before joining the army. Perhaps Lincoln thought surveying was something he could do that did not require the hard manual labor he so disliked. He was grateful to Calhoun for this job, as Offutt's business venture collapsed in debt, and Lincoln was left with nothing. He did this job part time, but he was thoroughly invested in the work, borrowing books to teach him the job. He learned geometry and trigonometry with the help of Mentor Graham, the local schoolmaster. Graham took a liking to Lincoln and would stay up with him through the night to teach him the principles. While Lincoln was in New Salem, he would learn not only mathematics but also rhetoric and Shakespeare, reading anything he could put his hands on. Graham's help would get Lincoln to pass the bar. Lincoln took his work seriously, measuring plots with exactness. He was by no means rich from his jobs and fell into debt that would follow him to Springfield. At one point, he was made to auction off his surveying equipment to ease his debt burden. A farmer named John Short bought the equipment for a large sum and gave Lincoln's tools back to him. Lincoln would keep the surveying job for three years, wandering Sangamon County from 1833 to 1835.

In New Salem, Lincoln would meet his first love. Ann Rutledge was the daughter of the New Salem innkeeper, and shortly after Lincoln's arrival, the pair sent a flurry of letters to each other. They studied grammar together under Mentor Graham and shared a love for poetry and reading. Both had similar outlooks on religion. Lincoln had never belonged to a church and had a simple belief in God, always searching for something more. Ann was much the same. In that time, it was not uncommon to have this simple outlook on religion. People were Christian but far from any organized church, believing their own way in their own home. Abraham and Ann were both searching for a higher spiritual calling and found each other.

In early 1834, Lincoln ran again for the state legislature. His time as storekeeper, postmaster, bartender and surveyor had brought him in contact with a great deal of the constituency, and Lincoln, owing to his ever-friendly nature, was able to win them over. The election still was close. Lincoln, as a Whig candidate, was up against a number of Democrats. Under the direction of his patron, John T. Stuart, who was also running for election in Sangamon County, Lincoln worked to get votes from Democrats who preferred him over Stuart. Close personal friendships with the people of New Salem gave him an edge. He won the election, as did the wily Stuart. This sent Lincoln down to Vandalia, where for the next three months he would be a backbench politician.

Lincoln had little influence on the legislature and didn't make any waves, but his time there was important for making him into a savvy politician. He rarely missed a session, taking great care to watch as seasoned lawmakers bickered back and forth on the floor. His mentor Stuart, a Whig leader, rallied support for bills while Abraham watched closely. Though his first time as an Illinois legislator was not marked by any Lincoln initiatives, it did convince him to continue his studies, and upon his return to New Salem, he prepared to pass the bar.

It was now the spring of 1834, and Lincoln was running his own general store, a business that was perpetually on the brink of bankruptcy, while continuing to work his many odd jobs. Abraham wore many hats, but none of them seemed to hold his passion. Law was the object of his desire—law and Ann Rutledge. Ann was engaged to a man who was considered to be something of a swindler. He had promised Ann that he would marry her upon his return from New York, but he had yet to return, and each day, Ann's affections for him dwindled. Abraham offered to go and collect her fiancé, but she refused to marry a man who would not visit her himself. She broke the engagement.

Lincoln was overjoyed, and the pair began a courtship. For a full year, they drew steadily closer to each other, neither wanting to rush their marriage, though both looked forward to it. They seemed destined for a long and happy life, but once again, tragedy came. While Lincoln was out surveying, typhus swept through the town of New Salem, and Ann fell ill. Hearing the news from a farmer, Abraham rushed home to find her on her deathbed. They shared a moment alone together, and a short time later, she died. Around that time, Lincoln's store partner died and left him with a $400 debt. Death had once more claimed those he loved, and the first great love of his life was, in his mind, forever tinged with grief.

Alone and deep in debt, Lincoln was eager to leave that town, now full of painful memories. He was briefly engaged to a Mary Owens, who had come to New Salem after her sister offered to bring her from Kentucky to be wed. Lincoln had agreed, mostly as a joke, and was horrified when she came. He tried to end the engagement, and after some time, an annoyed Mary agreed.

Abraham won reelection to the Illinois legislature and, during his second term, was admitted to the bar. While serving in the legislature in 1836, Abraham traveled to Albany, Whiteside County, Illinois—a small village on the Mississippi where a distant relation by the name of Stephen Hanks worked as a riverboat captain—at the invitation of John Wright and John Donovan to survey the village. It was a quick job for him; he set out a public square and seven blocks around it, divided along Meridian Street. In office, he pushed to lower property requirements for voting rights to give greater suffrage to poor white men. He was also concerned with infrastructure; in 1835, he helped pass a bill that began the digging of the Illinois-Michigan Canal, the long-planned project to pass through Chicago. Nationally, the ever-more-intricate issue of slavery was taking up more and more attention. Slavery had changed from the time of the Founding Fathers, as the mechanical cotton gin made plantation-style slavery more profitable. The institution of slavery grew to unimaginable size as massive plantations sprawled across the Southern states; nearly half the population of the South was in chains. Abraham, owing to his father's strict morality, had always opposed slavery. He staunchly sided with Free-Soil politics, which opposed slavery because the independent farmer could never compete with the plantation owner.

Lincoln and eight other representatives from Sangamon rallied to move the capital from Vandalia to Springfield. Their desire in moving the state capital was to make it more centrally located in Illinois, as well as to gain better access to waterways. These nine representatives were Whigs, and each was over six feet tall. They were dubbed the Long Nine by the papers. With their prodding, they made the capital move. Lincoln was the key man of the group, cleverly keeping the bill alive by tacking on amendments to get the votes it needed.

Moving from New Salem to Springfield, the town where he would live most of his life, Lincoln accepted the invitation from John Stuart to be his law partner. Stuart had just lost a congressional election. According to Lincoln's last law partner, William Herndon, Stuart was

> *still deeply absorbed in politics, and was preparing for the next canvass, in which he was finally successful—defeating the wily and ambitious Stephen A. Douglas. In consequence of the political allurements, Stuart did not give to the law his undivided time or the full force of his energy and intellect. Thus, more or less responsibility in the management of business and the conduct of cases soon fell on Lincoln.*

Facing this trial by fire, Lincoln conducted himself admirably, especially considering that he had been a lawyer for only about a year. It was Stuart's race that formally introduced Lincoln to the man he would face in nearly every battle he fought, those of elections and those for love: Stephen A. Douglas.

Lincoln and Douglas had met a few brief times before, the first time when Lincoln was a surveyor, but Stuart's loss served as a prelude to their political rivalry. Stephen's path was similar to Abraham's. He was born in Vermont; his father was a physician who died shortly after his birth. Like Lincoln, Douglas was a man of few prospects, training to be a cabinetmaker until he taught himself law. He came to Illinois in 1833 and was admitted to the bar the same year. Douglas quickly became a man of means and won renown as a lawyer. In 1835, at the same time as Lincoln, Douglas entered politics. He would live in Springfield for the next few years before moving to Chicago.

Douglas was a man of eternal compromise. A fierce voice for the betterment of his adopted state, he was willing to settle the most partisan debate with a well-reasoned deal that always gave something to Illinois. A lifelong Democrat, Douglas had a strange position on slavery. He always supported the free-state policies of Illinois, including free labor, but would inherit slaves from his father-in-law and used his plantation to finance his campaigns. Douglas was closely tied to the man who had given Abraham the surveying job, John Calhoun, and though Abraham was grateful for his job as deputy surveyor, in later years, Calhoun would become a political enemy of Lincoln's. It was Calhoun who pushed Douglas into running for

Congress. Calhoun was a pro-slavery Democrat who would become the surveyor-general of Kansas in the violent years of the Bleeding Kansas fighting. What Stuart was to Lincoln, Calhoun was to Douglas.

Upon arriving in Springfield in 1837, Lincoln, though with a job, had little else. He came to the general store owned by Joshua Speed looking to buy furniture and bedding on credit, as he did not have enough money to purchase anything. While Lincoln was meeting Speed for the first time, the shopkeeper already knew who he was, having watched a debate Lincoln participated in. Lincoln was dejected, according to Speed; debt and the dead weighed on his mind. Lincoln told Speed that he would either make it as a lawyer in the next year or fade away to nothing; moving to Springfield was his great gamble. Speed offered instead that Lincoln could live with him above the store. He and Lincoln would be roommates and share a bed for three years. Sharing of a bed was not uncommon on the frontier, as space was in short supply, and there was little expectation of privacy. Charles Hurst and William Herndon, both clerks for Speed, occasionally stayed with them. Though it was an odd pairing, Lincoln and Speed became the best of friends.

Their friendship was the closest of Lincoln's life. The two shared everything with each other: thoughts on politics, religion and romance. Lincoln relied on Speed during those dark early years in Springfield. They shared a love of reading and poetry, particularly Robert Burns. Together, they would dream of married life, though they recognized that reality would be quite different from their desires. Speed was something of a ladies' man and would take Lincoln with him to social functions. Where Abraham was shy and awkward, Speed was too charming for his own good. A number of scandals would surround his pursuits of women.

The first cornerstone of the new capitol building of Illinois was laid in 1837, with Lincoln in attendance. He was rising in prominence, becoming a leader of the Whigs. Notable names among the Illinois Whigs were Lincoln, John Stuart, Ninian Edwards Jr., John Harding, Jesse DuBois and O.H. Browning, while the Illinois Democrats were led by Stephen Douglas, W. Ewing, James Shields, Ebenezer Peck and John Calhoun. In the law office, Lincoln was handling most cases, as Stuart was increasingly focused on politics. Lincoln was good in a courtroom and could persuade a jury with his sharp mind and gentle manner. He gained many friends throughout Springfield, but besides Speed, he had no close friends.

The year 1837 was also an important one for Chicago, which became a city that year. Census records show that the city had 4,470 people in 1840, explosive growth from only a couple hundred in 1833. It was a wooden city and would flood with regularity, as the city was level with the lake. Democrat William Ogden was elected the first mayor over Whig John Kinzie. Chicago's first newspaper was founded in 1833 by a man named John Calhoun, though not the one Lincoln knew; the *Chicago Democrat* was soon sold to "Long" John Wentworth, a six-foot-six Vermont native who was owner and editor of the paper for many years. Men like Walter L. Newberry and William H. Brown had come to the city and established the first banks. From all over America, people came to the boomtown.

Abraham's life in Springfield settled into a rhythm. He worked hard at his law practice and in the state legislature. When Speed's store closed for the night, the Springfield lawyers would gather there around the furnace and tell each other stories. Abraham was a natural storyteller and was popular at these impromptu gatherings. Occasionally, Stephen Douglas would join. On weekends, Speed went to the parlors and parties of the Springfield elite, accepted into high society as his father owned a plantation. He would take the shy Lincoln with him.

Slowly, Lincoln became the de facto leader of the Whigs in the Illinois House of Representatives. Remembering the problems he had on the rivers of Illinois in his youth, he believed strongly in infrastructure spending, and the legislature frequently passed bills to improve roads, bridges and waterways. In this, he and Douglas were on the same side. Douglas introduced an infrastructure spending bill worth $7.5 million, which Abraham voted for. The bill was vetoed, but the legislature overrode it. In the end, the veto may have been better for Illinois. As the years passed, the only successful infrastructure project was the Illinois-Michigan Canal, while the others buried the state in debt.

In 1839, Stuart left for Washington to begin his first term as a congressman, and Abraham was left running the entire firm. Before, Stuart had been around to help somewhat; now, he was half a continent away. Lincoln was making around $1,000 annually at this time (roughly $26,000 in 2022 dollars). Being the Whig leader, Lincoln was invited to all sorts of Springfield society functions. In 1839, he attended one such party at the home of Ninian Edwards Jr.

Ninian was the son of the first and only governor of the territory of Illinois and had inherited his wealth. He was a famous man in the state, not least because he carried a gold cane and had a poor opinion of democracy. Politically, he was a Whig and knew Lincoln as a fellow member of the Long Nine. His wife, Elizabeth, was much younger than him, a perfect hostess and queen of the Springfield social scene. She had come from a wealthy slave-owning family out in Kentucky, the Todds.

Their magnificent party was held in celebration of the first legislative session convening in Springfield. Lincoln, the prime mover of placing the capital in Springfield, was the man of the hour, but he was not the only special guest that night. Elizabeth's sister had come from Kentucky to live with her for a time, visiting with relatives because she bickered constantly with her stepmother. Mary Todd was young, educated, intelligent, politically inclined and charming. She smiled and danced all night. The nervous and shy Lincoln asked her to dance, saying, "I should like to dance with you in the worst way." His dancing was awful, but she didn't mind. Mary had grown up in private boarding schools where everyone was required to speak French; she had learned to dance every fashionable style. He was angular, his limbs gangly; she was beautiful and elegant. She was undoubtedly from the Kentucky gentry, and Lincoln was a self-made man from the country.

Underneath the surface, however, they had a great deal in common. Both were Whigs and loved the poetry of Robert Burns. Mary knew Henry Clay, the famed Whig senator, who was a friend of the family. Clay was Abraham's hero, famous for cleverly devising the Missouri Compromise to save the Union—the man Abraham hoped would someday become president. Mary's cousins were all important Whigs, including John J. Hardin, the most popular Whig in Illinois and potentially president, had he not died in the Mexican-American War, and Lincoln's law partner, John T. Stuart, who was her favorite cousin growing up. For him to hear this list of family connections must have been quite impressive. While Abraham was stunned by the beautiful daughter of a wealthy political dynasty, Mary was eager to meet the man she had heard so much about. She knew about her cousin's new legal partner, a Whig who had worked closely with her brother-in-law to move the state capital.

They began a slow courtship, as Mary was the belle of the ball in Springfield. At one time, she was pursued by Stephen Douglas; some sources claim they were engaged, while others suggest it was a short courtship. Mary seems to have been set on Abraham from the time they met, at one point claiming that he would someday be president. He was less eager to marry, as he had reservations about how his life would change. Perhaps the death of Ann Rutledge still weighed on him. Abraham and Mary's relationship would take time. They would be engaged in late 1840.

In 1840, Lincoln was again reelected to the state legislature and was looking for an out from his law partnership with Stuart because he felt he had too much on his shoulders. He was arguing cases in front of the Illinois Supreme Court without guidance from his friend and partner. In March of that year, Speed's father had died, and Speed intended to return to administer his family plantation in Kentucky, perhaps because Ninian's sister Matilda had firmly rejected his advances. His departure upset Lincoln; Speed was the only close friend he had. Lincoln had planned to marry on January 1, 1841, but as the date approached and coincided with Speed's departure, his mood worsened. He had strong reservations about marrying; his letters to Speed are full of questions about married life. On the day of the wedding, Abraham called it off, leaving Mary at the altar.

Elizabeth was livid, and Abraham was no longer welcome in the home of the Edwards. Mary was heartbroken, thinking he was in love with someone else. The weight of all his troubles seemed to pull him down then. He dissolved his partnership with Stuart and was not renominated for a seat in the legislature. He did not seem to mind; the Whigs were in disarray, losing across the state. He was in such a downward spiral that people around him worried he was suicidal. Lincoln went to work as the junior partner of Stephen T. Logan, another of Mary's cousins. While he was once again a junior partner, at least he was not alone in the courtroom, as Logan had few political ambitions. He was an experienced lawyer who taught Abraham a good deal.

Lincoln visited the home of Speed later in 1841 and there regained his health and spirits. He was in such a state when he arrived that Speed had all the razors and rope hidden from him and had one of his slaves wait on him hand and foot. Speed was courting a woman named Fanny Henning, and Lincoln helped in the betrothal by engaging her uncle in a political debate while Speed proposed. Speed, eager for marriage, helped ease Abraham's own worries, and the letters Speed wrote to him were full of happy stories of his relationship. The rest of his life, Speed claimed that he was instrumental to Abraham's marriage with Mary, saying, "If I had not been married and happy—far more happy than I ever expected to be, He would not have married." Returning to Springfield, Abraham reentered political life.

In 1842, the Democrats in the legislature introduced a bill that forbade paying taxes in the state bank note, meaning all taxes had to be paid in hard gold and silver, a move aimed at closing the state bank (Illinois had gambled its financial future on the completion of the Illinois-Michigan Canal, taking on massive debt to do it, all handled by the state bank). This was beyond the means of most frontier farmers. When Lincoln had been the leader of the Whigs in the state legislature, he had worked against such efforts. Without

Stephen T. Logan

Left: John T. Stuart, Abraham's first law partner. Both he and Logan were cousins of Mary Todd and taught Abraham different aspects of the law. Stuart was instrumental in Lincoln's studies, giving him his books and encouraging him. Later, when Abraham passed the bar Stuart made him junior partner. *Abraham Lincoln Presidential Library and Museum.*

Right: Stephen T. Logan, Abraham's second law partner. Logan taught Lincoln how to argue cases in court. The partnership dissolved when Logan wanted to go into business with his son. Both Logan and Stuart later supported his political career. *Abraham Lincoln Presidential Library and Museum.*

the bank, the canal would fail, and Chicago would remain small. He and the Whigs jumped at this chance and harangued the Democrats over such a ridiculous law. Lincoln wrote a couple letters to the newspapers under the pen name Rebecca, poking fun at the Democrats in general and James Shields, the man who introduced the law, in particular. He showed Mary these letters, which she took immense joy in. Soon, more letters appeared in the papers, again from "Rebecca" and now far more inflammatory—but Lincoln did not write them. Confused, he was soon presented with a demand from Shields, who had gone to the newspaper and found out who wrote the first letter. He demanded a retraction, but Lincoln would not give it. Shields challenged him to a duel.

On September 27, 1842, Lincoln and Shields rode to Missouri, where dueling was legal. As the challenged party, Lincoln had his choice of weapons, picking the cavalry saber. At six foot four, Lincoln had a massive height advantage and could reach farther than his opponent, which he demonstrated when he absentmindedly reached up and cut a switch off a tree. The casual display unnerved Shields's friends. Before the duel could begin, Mary Todd's cousin John Hardin and Democrat Revel English arrived and offered to present the case to an impartial judge. Shields's friends then told Lincoln that his aggressive demands were withdrawn, something Shields had not said, and Lincoln apologized for the "Rebecca" letters. Later, Lincoln found out that the more raucous letters had been written by Mary Todd as vengeance for Shields's unwanted affections toward a friend of hers. It is possible that Mary sent her cousin Hardin to stop the duel, feeling guilty about putting Lincoln in that situation.

Lincoln was ashamed of his behavior, of letting his emotions run away with him, and took great care to never mention it again. When an officer asked him during the Civil War if it was "true… that he had fought a duel for the sake of the lady by your side," Lincoln responded, "I do not deny it. But if you desire my friendship, you will never mention it again." Shields would fight in the Civil War for the Union, and when he was wounded in a battle against Stonewall Jackson, Lincoln offered to promote him to major general, ending any ill feeling.

Abraham and Mary were reconciled. She was grateful for him facing a duel for her sake, recognizing that it was her fault he had faced possible death. Hardin pulled a number of tricks to get the couple back together. At a dinner party, Hardin took everyone but Mary on a carriage ride, leaving her fuming on the side of the road. However, Lincoln suddenly showed up in his own carriage and took her along; she was elated. Lincoln was resolved to court Mary, even though he was still nervous. Marrying her would keep his honor intact. For her part, Mary had long desired to marry him. He proposed in the fall. Mary, though ecstatic, kept their engagement a secret so that she would not be embarrassed should it fall through again. They were alone together a number of times at the home of mutual friends in the months to follow.

On November 4, 1842, Lincoln burst into the home of Reverend Charles Dresser during breakfast and told him, "I want to get hitched tonight." The minister checked his engagements and told Lincoln he was available. Lincoln went to the jewelers and bought a gold band with the inscription: "A.L. To Mary, Nov. 4, 1842. Love is Eternal." Mary told her sister that she would wed Lincoln that night at Elizabeth's home. Elizabeth was understandably upset at having to organize a party on such short notice. She also did not care much for Abraham after he had left Mary at the altar before. That night, in the mansion of the Edwards, Abraham and Mary were wed. They rented a small room at the Globe Tavern, a stagecoach stop, not having the money for a honeymoon. There they would have their first child, Robert Todd Lincoln, almost nine months after their wedding.

Marriage took some getting used to for both of them. Mary was born into one of the wealthiest families in Kentucky and had come to expect certain luxuries; she had been waited on hand and foot. She was now living in a tavern with a man who had been raised in a log cabin. If she thought her marriage would be glamorous, those early years quickly proved her wrong. For his part, Abraham had to persuade supporters that he wasn't a member of the Stuart-Todd-Edwards dynasty of elitist Whigs, that he was still the same man he ever was. Abraham would talk to the people who came through the tavern when Mary was cross with him. Soon after Robert's birth, the Lincolns purchased a one-story home in Springfield from Reverend Dresser. The home was small, but it suited the family. In the backyard stable was a cow that provided milk for them. It was the only house Lincoln would ever own.

Abraham had run for Congress in 1843 but lost the Whig nomination to John Hardin. His law partner, Logan, decided to go into business with his son in 1844. Suddenly without a job, Lincoln established his own law firm and took on a junior partner, William H. Herndon. He had known Herndon from his first days in Springfield, as they both roomed above Speed's store. Herndon made good money working as a clerk, but once he married, he knew he would need more to support his family. Abraham convinced him to become a lawyer. He wanted Herndon as his next legal partner because of his good organizational skills. Lincoln was bad at keeping detailed legal records. Herndon would pass the bar, working during the day and studying at night by reading law at the Logan & Lincoln law office. As the junior partner of the firm, Herndon was tasked with all research that Lincoln might need, as well as overseeing the students who read law at their firm.

This partnership would last until the end of Abraham's life. Lincoln's law career was in his own hands, and he worked whichever cases he chose. Herndon was totally devoted to him, happy to run errands. They were most frequently engaged in debt collection, arguing for both debtors and collectors. Lincoln frequently argued cases before the Illinois Supreme Court, as well as federal district and circuit courts. Herndon typically argued before lower courts. Both partners shared an equal amount of the paperwork, though Herndon did much of the research. In a few short years, the firm was one of the most prestigious in Springfield, handling over two hundred cases a year.

Lincoln's new next-door neighbors on Ninth Street were the Gourleys. James Gourley was a shoemaker and handyman. Later on in life, he would be a sheriff. The Gourleys and Lincolns got along well. Abraham would occasionally come to their house to borrow milk when his own cow went dry, dressed in old clothes and slippers. Their children were friends for life. Gourley told Herndon, "Bob and my boy…used to harness up my dog and they would take him into the woods and get nuts." He also remembered that Lincoln would always read out loud, most frequently from the Bible.

In his interview with Herndon, James Gourley said that Abraham was always kind and that no one was a better friend than Mary to them, even when she "got the devil in her." Visitors and passersby noted several occasions where Mary chased Abraham around the yard with a broomstick, once with a knife, shouting abuse at him for his forgetfulness, such as the time he got the wrong cut of meat. Abraham would often just leave the home for a few hours when his wife was on a rampage. Her ire was not reserved for her husband, and the Lincolns had a hard time keeping domestic help. When one servant asked for a raise, Mary fired her. Abe offered to pay her a raise under the table, but Mary overheard them and stormed in, firing the maid for good and scolding her husband. She would often haggle with the peddlers who came door to door over the price of vegetables, frugal with the money they had. She had been raised in a family with many slaves and was now cooking and cleaning by herself. With the money she saved, she would buy fabric to make their clothes. The home was a step up from the tavern, but it fell short of her desires. It took some adjustment for her, and her husband's carefree ways and country manners didn't help.

The Lincolns lived on $1,500 a year. They were not struggling, but Mary wanted greater financial security. In 1846, Edward Lincoln was born, and soon after, Abraham was elected to the U.S. House of Representatives as a Whig. Abraham and Mary had been married for four years and were learning to get along with each other. Life would only get easier for them as Mary's large, wealthy and ageing family began dying, and she occasionally received inheritances from affectionate aunts.

The family of four began packing for their trip to Washington to support Abraham as he served in the House of Representatives. Before he went to the seat of American government, Abraham was chosen to serve as a representative at the 1847 Rivers and Harbors Convention in Chicago. He went to Chicago for the first time in his life and began his long climb into the spotlight.

Chapter *2*

ONTO THE STAGE

A rriving in Chicago for the first time in his life, Abraham was just a face in the crowd, one of five thousand people attending the River and Harbor Convention of 1847. Chicago at that time had twenty-five thousand people, continuing its unmatched growth. No railroads came into the city. The thousands of delegates arrived by coach or boat; ferries offered reduced rates for conventiongoers. As would be commonplace with future Chicago conventions, there wasn't enough space for everyone. The attendees would pack hotels, inns and private homes. Some rented rooms on riverboats; some even camped out in the streets and surrounding prairie.

What greeted those thousands was a wooden town, built on a swamp. Chicago had been a city for a decade, growing so fast that they said the buildings changed from week to week. Because of the speed of construction, new architectural styles were necessary. The balloon frame style, conceived by George W. Snow, made it possible to build wooden structures quickly. The style was adopted throughout the United States and was the first of Chicago's contributions to architecture. Still, to leave the prim and proper Springfield, home of Illinois's wealth and politics, and enter the gloomy, kerosene-lit, swampy Chicago must have been a shock for Lincoln.

The *Chicago Journal* wrote of his arrival,

> *Abraham Lincoln, the only Whig representative in Congress from this State, we are happy to see is in attendance upon the Convention. This is his first visit to the commercial emporium of the State, and we have no doubt*

his visit will impress him more deeply.…We expect much from him as a representative in Congress.

Many in attendance thought Lincoln's appearance bizarre. Tall and angular, Congressman-elect Lincoln showed up in "a short-waisted thin swallow-tailed coat, short vest of the same material, thin pantaloons scarcely coming down to his ankles, straw hat, pair of brogans, and woolen socks," for which he was dubbed Old Abe. He was no headline attraction at that convention; he was hardly known outside Sangamon County, and many Whig celebrities had come to voice their grievances against President Polk. Nineteen states had sent official delegations, and in attendance were such notables as newspaper mogul Horace Greeley, Edward Bates (who would be Lincoln's attorney general) and future president Millard Fillmore. Lincoln's idol, Senator Henry Clay, was not in attendance but sent a strongly worded letter that was read aloud to the assembly.

The convention was a protest organized by Congressman "Long" John Wentworth of Chicago and William Hall, in response to President Polk's veto of a congressional funding bill that would have improved the waterways of the inland United States. Polk felt that since the bill did not pertain to national defense or trade, the states should pay any money that went to their infrastructure. Northern states had long campaigned for federal assistance in improving transportation through the region but had not received any. The thousands of delegates from counties across the nation came to show how unpopular the veto was. Infrastructure was the cornerstone of Lincoln's political platform, ever since he had been stranded on the milldam in New Salem. His first campaign for state legislature was run on that premise.

Water was the highway of the day, moving people and goods from lakes to rivers to canals to creeks. Steamboats were the fastest transport available to most people. Railways were only starting to be built, mainly in the East. The newest development in American infrastructure was the Erie Canal, a three-hundred-mile manmade river that allowed transport from the Great Lakes to New York City and, from there, to the world. There were millions of Americans whose goods were cut off from global markets because of the conditions of roads and waterways. Chicago was chosen as the location of the convention to highlight the Illinois-Michigan Canal, near completion, which would connect the Great Lakes to the Mississippi and, from there, to the Gulf of Mexico, emphasizing to the administration the influence infrastructure had on trade.

At six foot six, Long John Wentworth towered over everyone, including Abraham Lincoln. A giant of early Chicago, Wentworth bought the city's first newspaper, the *Democrat*, was elected to Congress five times and was mayor of Chicago twice. He and Lincoln were fast friends. *A.T. Andreas,* History of Chicago, *vol. 1.*

The convention met for three days in July. Lincoln, though not vital to these proceedings, was acquainted with many powerful figures of the age. His only notable moment was a short rebuttal on behalf of the Whigs to David Field, a New York Democrat in favor of only limited spending on rivers. Though brief, Lincoln's rebuttal was memorable, calling for all members to unite as a "band of brothers" and work toward a compromise, not spending too much money but also financing all necessary projects. In Greeley's coverage of the event, he noted that Lincoln spoke "briefly and happily." Although his one speech did not change the course of the convention, nor were his points adopted as policy, Lincoln could consider it a success based on the mere fact that Horace Greeley mentioned him favorably. Greeley ran the *New-York Tribune* and was a powerful Whig voice. His paper was the most read in the country, even in proslavery strongholds. Lincoln also got a first look at his soon-to-be colleagues of the Thirtieth Congress, such as the giant John Wentworth. At the end of the three days, the convention refuted all Polk's reasons for his veto, and everyone went on their way.

Returning to Springfield, Lincoln packed up his family and prepared for the journey to Washington. The small family of four was eager for their big trip to the capital of the nation. They were not planning to live there, as Abraham had long held the belief that a congressman should serve only one term before allowing other men of his party to take his place. It was a common idea at the time, aimed at allowing new people and new ideas to be heard in Congress. In his earlier failure to get the Whig nomination, losing to Hardin, Lincoln had come to the understanding that he would be next in line. He did not follow Hardin directly into Congress, but he was elected a short time later. Lincoln, having finally attained his goal, stood by his convictions and did not seek reelection.

It was lucky for Lincoln that this was his plan, because his time in Congress was not as successful as he hoped it would be. The major issue of the legislative session was the Mexican-American War. The expansionist President Polk sought to annex the new and controversially independent Republic of Texas into the Union. Though Texas had claimed its independence by capturing President Santa Anna, Mexico deposed the disgraced general and refused to acknowledge Texas's independence, though there was little Mexico could do to bring Texas back into the fold at that time. The republic was eager to join the United States and was annexed into the Union on December 29, 1845. Mexico did not recognize the annexation, and the road to war began.

President Polk ordered General Zachary Taylor to take a small army of three thousand and wander around the south of Texas until they were attacked. Years later, Ulysses S. Grant, a quartermaster present in this force, wrote that they were clearly looking to provoke a battle. The American forces were attacked in due time, and Polk went to Congress demanding a declaration of war, claiming that American troops had been killed on American soil. Congress obliged. Grant thought the war was a despicable land grab, a belief he shared with his future commander-in-chief.

Lincoln's congressional career began on December 6, 1847, with the war in full swing. He was the only Whig from Illinois; the party was struggling to maintain popularity. Beside him sat four-time congressman from Chicago Long John Wentworth. Due to Abraham's natural charm, the pair became fast friends. Abraham joined the Whigs in opposing the War Democrats and the conflict they had provoked. He was in good company, with former president John Quincy Adams and Senator Henry Clay leading the opposition to the war. Abraham introduced eight resolutions for Congress to approve that demanded Polk give the exact location where the American blood had been shed. These resolutions were political suicide for Lincoln.

He aimed to prove that Polk had lied to Congress and deliberately started the war, but the Democrats called him unpatriotic, and the Whigs began thinking that debating the war would hurt their chances politically. They had opposed the war, but as it raged and became popular with the American public, they backed down from their rhetoric. Lincoln would not back down. Congress did not adopt any of his so-called Spot Provisions, and he became known as "spotty Lincoln" and lampooned in newspapers throughout the country. Douglas argued for continuation of the war, and a veteran of that war, Jefferson Davis, called for the annexation of the Yucatán as well as all of northern Mexico. Lincoln was against any further fighting.

In Illinois, Lincoln's popularity fell to an all-time low. His political base was grassroots, loving their simple backwoods lawyer, but the support for the war was also grassroots. The people of his district found their patriotism more appealing than their congressman. The Whig Party in Springfield faced mass desertion, and Herndon warned Lincoln that he had no chance at reelection. Had he run again, he would have been walloped.

The Mexican-American War ended in early 1848 in a complete victory for the United States, shaping the modern border between the two countries. Manifest Destiny had been achieved; the United States stretched from sea to sea. Texas, California, Arizona and New Mexico joined the Union as states or territories. However, instead of solving America's problems, this only made the stakes higher.

Suddenly, the tension over the question of slavery intensified. Ever since the Constitution was ratified, a solution to the problem had been kicked down the road by a series of compromises. Part of the reason for the delay was a perceived absolute need to maintain the ratio of free states to slave. The admission of Texas threw the balance out of whack. Storm clouds were brewing. Debates on the future of slavery raged through Congress, taking up most of the legislative agenda—and on this issue, the Whigs could not quite unify. There was a fear that territory taken in the Mexican-American War would quickly become slave states and that the ratio between free and slave would be thrown out of balance forever. It was hoped that California would balance out Texas, but beyond that, there were not enough new free states to balance out the war gains.

Shortly before the first session of Congress adjourned, Lincoln witnessed John Quincy Adams, a titan of Whig politics and leader of the resistance to the Polk administration, collapse on the floor of the House. He would pass away two days later in an anteroom of the Capitol building. His would be the first in a series of deaths of key Whig leaders who held the party together. The party would struggle to replace its founding generation; the caliber of the Whig founders went unmatched.

On the family front, Lincoln found himself alone in Washington fairly quickly, for though Mary and the children, Robert and Eddie, came with him to the capital, they soon left. Most congressmen did not bring their wives with them, preferring the capital's many brothels. The wives who did come were well versed in Washington etiquette. Mary found the city uncomfortable. It was swampy and smelly, and she did not get along with its people. Raised in the Kentucky gentry, she had looked down on the people of Illinois, but she soon found the eastern socialites looked down on her for coming from the West, thinking her some country hick. Unable to stand it, Mary left with the children for Kentucky, where she would stay with her family, people she could get along with most of the time.

On July 4, 1848, the cornerstone of the Washington Monument was laid. President Polk led a solemn ceremony, dedicating the monument to the nation's first president. In attendance was all of Congress, including Lincoln, as well as many foreign dignitaries and the widows of two of the Founding Fathers, Dolley Madison and Elizabeth Hamilton. It was a beautiful ceremony, one of the last things that the states did together for the next decade and a half. The coming fifties would be a time of political disunity and partisanship.

After the dedication of the Washington Monument, Congress ended its summer session. Lincoln spent his summer campaigning in the presidential election for General Zachary Taylor, the conquering hero of the Mexican-American War. The whole campaign was odd, as Taylor never had political aspirations or close ties to either party; he rode exclusively on his impressive military record. The Whigs had chosen him to be their man, but it was to be their last push. Before Lincoln set out to canvas the Northeast, Mary and the boys rejoined him. Campaigning consisted of a speaking tour. A small group of politicians went town to town, and their speeches took all day—the main speaker alone could go on for three hours. Abraham toured for nearly two months in his most intense speaking engagement to date. Along the way, he learned what it took to run a national campaign.

After stumping for Taylor throughout New England, Lincoln went with his family to Niagara Falls. Its natural beauty so stunned him that he wrote a natural history essay and a companion spiritual piece about it. The natural world was often a theme of Abraham's private writings, as he found peace in the landscape. Later, when he was president, he managed to give some protection to the natural world when he signed the Yosemite Grant into law, creating the nucleus of what would become the national park system. Boarding a steamboat from Buffalo, the Lincolns headed back to Springfield by way of Chicago. It was a pleasant cruise through the Great Lakes, one thousand miles to Chicago and plenty of time to reconnect as a family.

Abraham and Mary had been married for six years and had mostly learned to get along. While separated, they wrote to each other often, he about the matters of Congress and she about the children. She found her happiness in watching Robert play, and she pampered him. Their finances had improved greatly. When they were first married, Abraham was earning $1,500 a year. Returning to Springfield, he was making approximately $2,000. Additionally, Mary's father had given them an eighty-acre plot in Kentucky. Mary did not need to penny-pinch any more, and as family inheritances came in, she was able to make their home more to her tastes, slowly refining their rugged surroundings. However, at home, Mary remained prone to mood swings, and when she felt her husband was not fulfilling his duties, she would unleash tirades of abuse at him, once or twice striking him so hard it cut him. At these times, Abraham would leave the house and walk until she had time to cool off.

The pleasant lakeside cruise landed in Milwaukee on October 4, 1848, and the family had a nice day out before returning aboard their ship, arriving in Chicago the next day. Records show that the family stayed in the Sherman House Hotel for a few days before heading home to Springfield. This was Abraham's second time in Chicago and, for the rest of his family, their first. Fredrika Bremer, a Swedish writer and traveler, remarked that it was the ugliest city in America at that time, but the people were "most agreeable and delightful-good people, handsome and intellectual; people to live with." Chicago's connections to industry and raw goods grew with every day. In the year since Lincoln's last visit, the city had already installed its first railway and opened the Illinois-Michigan Canal, connecting the Great Lakes to the Gulf of Mexico. The canal was ninety-six miles long and dug entirely by hand. It was sixty feet wide and only six feet deep; barges were towed along by pack animals. Digging the canal had placed terrible financial strain on the young state government. Illinois had taken out two rounds of massive domestic and foreign loans, and the debt almost bankrupted the state in 1842. Despite the many troubles that the creation of the canal caused, its completion placed Chicago and Illinois in the black. By selling lands on either side of the canal and collecting tolls set on goods per pound per mile, the state quickly made its money back. After completion of the canal, all loans were repaid in five years. In the ten-year period after its opening, 5.5

million bushels of wheat, 27 million pounds of pork and 26 million bushels of corn went through the canal and raised over $1 million for the state and bondholders. The Galena and Chicago Union rail line connected the vast resources of the Midwest to this transportation network. Walter Newberry was the first president of the line, and William H. Brown sat on its board. Within two years, Chicago would be the central hub of northern railroads. Mary, in particular, loved the city. It was still growing, but it had all the shops and boutiques that she was well disposed toward. The first synagogue would open in 1851, four years after the congregation began, a humble beginning to a thriving community today. Of all the cities of Illinois, Chicago was the only one on its way to becoming a metropolis.

For that reason, Stephen Douglas had moved there with his new wife, Martha Martin. Her father died shortly after their wedding and left Douglas with a plantation, along with one hundred slaves. Eager to keep his ownership of the plantation a secret while using it to pay for his career, he only went there for a few short visits. A wealthy man and perhaps the most famous senator in the entire country, Douglas moved south of Chicago proper, buying up large tracts of land outside the city limits, which he would later donate to schools and churches. The move was a strange one, as his support lay in the south of the state, while Chicago belonged to the Whigs, but Douglas saw the city had a future.

In Chicago and preparing to go home, Lincoln was called upon to give a speech at a Whig rally. Though given only six hours to prepare, he gave a speech to an eager crowd. The crowd was so large that the planned facility was abandoned, and the rally reconvened in a nearby park. Lincoln spoke for two hours, impressing on the people that should Taylor lose, the Free-Soil North would come under attack. His speech was well received, for though the Whig party in Illinois was dying, in Chicago, free enterprise was held onto more firmly than ever. His speech made him a celebrity, to the point that Chicagoans would harass him to give speeches whenever he was in town.

The Lincoln family soon left Chicago, heading south to a home they had not seen in a year. Their house had been rented out while they were away, all their private things tucked away in one room. They arrived home on October 10, and store records show that they settled back in, buying a few things to spruce up the home. His first session of Congress had not gone as Lincoln had hoped, and he was eager to return to his law firm. William Herndon had been placed in a situation much like the one Lincoln had been in with Stuart: a junior lawyer taking on all the firm's cases while the senior partner was away in Congress. When Stuart left Lincoln for Congress,

Herndon later wrote, Lincoln felt betrayed in having to run the office himself. When Lincoln did this to Herndon, Herndon gladly accepted that Lincoln had places to be and that he had to keep the office running until his partner got back. Herndon did not complain; he was happy to do whatever Abraham required of him. It was the kind of loyalty that Lincoln inspired in many people he met. Herndon had kept up regular correspondence with Lincoln while he was away, giving him information on the political landscape. Abraham knew that he would have a challenging time running for any political office. The Whig party in Illinois was fading. His political career was most likely dead.

In the election of 1848, Abraham voted straight-ticket Whig, though Illinois did not. General Taylor won in a close election. Although the Democrats won Illinois, electoral results show that the northeastern corner of the state, centered around Chicago, voted Free-Soil, a party led by former president Martin Van Buren. The Free-Soil Party believed in ending the expansion of slavery in all new states. More protectionist than abolitionist, they were reviled in the South. Chicago stood against slavery and was only waiting for a party that could take these goals to Washington. The Free-Soil Party would continue on for years as a small national party, a boogeyman in the South, before joining forces with a party that could win it all. It was accepted at the time that upon assuming office, the president would give political appointments to the people who had worked to get him elected. Referred to as the spoils system, this was a patronage network that filled positions with those loyal to the president's backers, not those with merit. For all his hard work on the Taylor campaign, Lincoln had hoped for an office somewhere in Illinois, but all he was offered was an appointment to be secretary of the Territory of Oregon. Mary absolutely refused to move there, and Abraham turned the post down.

Mary and the children remained home when Abraham returned to Washington to finish his term in office. The first half of his term had been disastrous, and in the second half, he introduced no major legislation. He voted repeatedly for the Wilmot Proviso, which called for a ban on slavery in the newly conquered territories, but it never passed.

Disillusioned, Abraham returned to Springfield; he would not return to politics for six years. Settling down, the Lincolns reconnected with the Gourley family, and although Mary would occasionally fly into a rage at her forgetful husband, they were happy and well off. In May 1849, Abraham was able to give a loan of $500. Just a few short years ago, such a loan would have constituted half of his yearly income, but by 1849, Lincoln had a large nest egg and was making a fair amount from his law firm. It helped that he had simple tastes. The family had received a large windfall when Mary's father, Robert Todd, died. In his will, he left them $1,000, around half of Abraham's annual income.

Also in May, Abraham received a long-awaited letter from the U.S. Patent Office, officially granting him U.S. patent 6,469. It was for a mechanical device that he had worked on in his spare time. A set of bellows was attached to the side of a boat that would lift the boat off any shoal; the memory of his time stranded on the rivers of Illinois evidently never lost his interest. Submarines work on the same principle. There are some doubts as to whether Lincoln's rudimentary invention would have worked, as a large amount of energy is needed to lift a boat out of water. As of this writing, he is the only president to hold a patent.

Lincoln's patent was part of a global trend. The early 1800s was a time of invention. The first Industrial Revolution had changed the way people lived on a scale never seen before, allowing for goods to be manufactured and shipped across the globe in record time. There were constant improvements to existing machines, oftentimes by people in the countryside. Lincoln's own patent, number 6,469, reveals the astonishing number of patents awarded by the government in a mere fifty-nine years.

As 1850 approached, Abraham joined the Eighth Circuit Court in order to make a living. The courts were quite different at that time. A portion of the population was assigned to a district. A court was a group of judges, lawyers and bail bondsmen who went around that district from town to town and heard cases. They did not sit in one courthouse. When court was in session, all those from miles around came to have their complaints heard. A court coming was a big event in any town; so many people came that it felt like a fair. The atmosphere was none too different from a fair, either. People would watch from the gallery as lawyers argued their cases, cheering and booing. Shops would spring up outside the courthouse, selling wares to spectators. Then the court would pack up and go to another town.

Time on the court was long; from February to June, then September to December they traveled. Lincoln was gone from home half the year. Mary would live on her own, raising the children and running the house. The money he made was good for the family, but his time away was not. The family had a number of servants, but these could never stand Mary for long. On one occasion, the relative of a maid Mary had shouted out of the house came to Abraham, demanding an apology. Abraham calmed him, saying, "Friend, can't you endure this one wrong done to you by a mad woman for our friendship's sake while I have had to bear it without complaint for lo these many years." The man was moved to pity, and he assured Abraham that they would remain friends. Dennis Hanks's daughter Harriet Hanks stayed with them for a year while attending school in Springfield and would help out around the house. She only lasted a year, as Mary thought she was a dirt-poor hick and would pour abuse on her. Harriet was the only member of Abraham's family Mary ever met. When Mary had need of extra help, she went to the Gourleys. James would do odd jobs for them when Abraham was away, chopping firewood and fixing up the house, a handyman for the family. James, one time, went and found a carriage for Mary's purchase, and she would hire young men from the neighborhood to take her where she wanted to go. They were paid ten or fifteen cents a ride, depending on where they were going. Another time, when Mary was frightened by hooligans in the area, Mr. Gourley spent the night at the Lincoln home, guarding the house in case of an incident. Nothing happened.

After his first session on the circuit court, Abraham returned home to find that Eddie was sick; he had fallen ill months earlier, and he was not recovering. For a full month, doctors were called in to treat him, as Abraham and Mary watched helplessly. For all their effort, Eddie died on February 1, 1850. The disease is generally thought to be tuberculosis, but there is debate today about other possible illnesses. Abraham and Mary were despondent after Eddie's death. The funeral took place at First Presbyterian Church; the service was done by Dr. James Smith. After the service, Abraham stayed to question Smith and found that the pastor had answers for his doubts. Smith had had his own doubts in his youth and worked his way through them with study. Having found his faith, Smith published a two-volume work of Christian apologism called *The Christian's Defence* [sic]. Smith gave Abraham a copy, and he found the book answered many of his questions. Meanwhile, Mary began her long, slow drift toward Spiritualism and mysticism rather innocently, as her husband rented a pew in Smith's church for the family and she attended each Sunday, looking for solace. The Lincoln family grew close to its pastor, though Abraham was often away.

Abraham himself had a long history of depression; each loss in his life stayed with him, weighing on his mind. He was a soft and kindhearted man who cared deeply for others. When the people he loved died, he would not lie in bed like Mary but rather carried on his routine, wearier and more worn down than ever. His depression would eat away at him at times, and he would grow thin. There were months when he barely ate. He loved to tell jokes and stories, but when not at a party, a melancholy attached itself to him.

After Eddie was buried, Abraham had to leave to get back to the circuit and earn his family money. Mary was alone shortly after the death of her child. Robert was still with her, and she fretted over him more than ever. She relied on the Gourleys for support, incapable of all but the most basic tasks in the months after Eddie's death.

Riding from town to town and working on cases, occupied with the tedium of it all, Abraham could at least distract himself with his work. He was traveling with a number of judges and lawyers, birds of a feather, and many of them became lifelong friends. While on the circuit, Lincoln would stay in various inns set aside for the traveling courts. Since there was never enough space, the members of the court had to occasionally sleep two to a bed and twenty to a room. Tall and gangly, Abraham only rarely found things suited for people of his stature while traveling. When he once found a bathtub large enough for himself, he immediately got in and bathed. The number of people who would descend on a town was often too much for the residents to accommodate.

A particularly good friend was Judge David Davis. Davis was fascinated with Lincoln's storytelling power and held him in high esteem. He had Lincoln tell stories in downtime, of which there was a fair amount. However, Davis's opinion of Lincoln did not give him a bias when it came to court cases. Of the eighty-seven juryless cases Lincoln argued before Davis, Davis ruled in his favor forty times.

Judge David Davis, friend of Abraham and later mentor of Robert. Davis had a high opinion of both but was on bad terms with Mary. He was appointed to the Supreme Court by Abraham, though he would retire to run for senator. He remained close to the Lincoln family all his life. *Library of Congress, Brady-Handy Photograph Collection, LC-DIG-cwpbh-02279.*

Lincoln, who was being reimbursed for travel expenses, would often pad out his mileage. It was hard, in those days, to say exactly how far one place was from another, and his inflated mile count may have come from his giving a rough estimate of how far he had gone. However, it is possible that Honest Abe was not always as honest as presumed. While other members of the traveling court went home for the weekends, Abraham often stayed in taverns.

Lincoln returned from the circuit in April, staying in Springfield for the summer months with his still grieving family. Mary soon became pregnant. While back home, Lincoln and Herndon worked a number of small cases.

In July 1850, Lincoln went to Chicago to represent Charles Hoyt, who was being sued by a man named Parker for patent infringement. Lincoln's own patent gave him an interest in the complexities of patent law. The case would last weeks as several appeals for a new trial were granted, dragging out the case. While Lincoln was in Chicago, the shocking news came: President Taylor had died, and Vice President Millard Fillmore had been sworn in. Taylor had won his campaign in the Northeast and South, a slave-owning Whig backed by opposing interests; his term was marked by few new initiatives. With his death, the presidency went to a Northern Whig. Factionalism and partisanship grew as regional interests began to clash. Fillmore would be the last Whig president, and the party would collapse soon after his administration. The death of Taylor would prove to be the second key loss the Whigs faced in the turbulent years leading up to the war.

Grand eulogies were given in Washington, and Lincoln was off on the sidelines, unable, like his peers, to use the funeral to gain national attention. He was not yet so completely turned off of politics that he did not want to promote himself as those in Washington did. But he was not entirely left out, for the Whigs in Chicago wanted to have as grand a sendoff for Taylor as the eastern cities, to prove themselves their equal. Lincoln was chosen to do the eulogy as soon as his protracted legal case ended.

Lincoln gave the eulogy on July 25 in the Chicago courthouse, to a large crowd. The eulogy focused on the Mexican-American War, which Lincoln had so disastrously opposed. Taylor's great battles and unflappable nature were extolled for the crowd, making Taylor seem like the hero of the North. In reality, Taylor's presidency was little more than a placeholder. He was not a politician, and his administration did not produce any significant initiatives. The Whigs did not choose him for ideological purity nor faithfulness to their ideals; he was the only man in America they could get elected, based almost entirely on his war record. Lincoln spoke to a crowd one thousand strong and was able to capture some of the limelight. Chicago, at least, had not forgotten Lincoln.

Lincoln left Chicago later that week and returned to Springfield. He spent only a short time at home, then left to ride the circuit with Davis and others. The money he had earned in Chicago was more than he made riding the circuit, but he did not want to move there. He was away the entire fall, Mary pregnant and raising Robert on her own, having seen little of her husband throughout the year. Lincoln was away for their eighth anniversary. On December 21, William was born, the third Lincoln boy.

Twenty-seven days later, Abraham's father, Thomas, died. Thomas had not attended Abraham's wedding (though it was so sudden, he could not have known about it), nor did he meet his grandchildren or even his daughter-in-law. Thomas saw little of his son after he left. Abraham would visit if the court took him nearby, but he never stayed long. The last few years, Abraham's father and stepbrother made appeals to him for money, asking him to ease the family's financial burden. Abraham always sent the money, though he thought his stepbrother was lazy and pocketing what he sent, but he did not bring his family to see his parents. Their relationship had been difficult and combative, yet Thomas had passed his convictions down. Abraham resented his father for being a simple carpenter and making him do farm work, but this would later boost his political career. Thomas was buried on the family plot. Abraham did not attend the funeral, his excuse being that Mary was ill. With the death of his father, Abraham was all that remained from the Kentucky farm.

Chapter 3

THE ITINERANT LAWYER

In the year 1850, it seemed that the entire issue of slavery in America was resolved. Stephen Douglas, working with Henry Clay, introduced five bills to the Senate floor. These bills shrank Texas in return for assuming the state's public debt, admitted California into the Union, created the territories of New Mexico and Utah, banned the slave trade in Washington, D.C., and obligated the Northern states to return runaway slaves. Just a few months earlier, such a compromise would have been impossible, as President Taylor had been set against any compromise on the question of slavery, but upon assuming office, Millard Fillmore proved willing to bury the hatchet.

The free states won big in the Compromise of 1850. The slave state Texas could no longer claim so much territory to its west, and California was admitted free to even the balance. Additionally, gold had been discovered in California soon after the Mexican-American War ended, causing a gold rush. The gold would later help fund the Union war effort. There was now one large slave state and one large free state. The practice of slavery still existed in Washington, D.C., but the slave trade was banned, perhaps the first step to eradicating slavery from the nation's capital. The territories of New Mexico and Utah were placed on the fast track to statehood, with popular sovereignty deciding if slavery would exist in those states, and since no cash crop would grow in the arid climate, the free states could rest assured that two new free states would enter the Union soon.

Yet things were not all rosy for free states; after all, it was a compromise. Slave states got a much stronger Fugitive Slave Act that penalized law enforcement in any state $1,000 for failing to help capture a runaway slave. The act also gave a six-month prison sentence or $1,000 fine to anyone who aided a fugitive slave. The compromise also alleviated all the public debt of Texas, which it had taken on in its war for independence. Instead of arid New Mexico and Utah, slaveholders looked north to the fertile lands of Kansas and Nebraska to be the next home to slavery.

While the compromise was widely accepted by the people of America in the hope of ending the war of words between the states, both sides pointed to things they hated. The Fugitive Slave Law outraged the North. Those who opposed slavery were now, by law, required to perpetuate the system. Slave owners, on the other hand, were furious that the capital would no longer permit the slave trade; their hold on the city was being taken away.

On the whole, the compromise appeared to have ended the crisis between states. Henry Clay once again delivered a deal that saved the nation. The compromise delayed the conflict that was brewing by eleven years. In those years, the North would build thousands of miles of railways, hundreds of factories and grow in population by millions. At the time of the war, New York City alone produced as many industrial goods as the entire Confederacy. The South, meanwhile, was lethargic during this time, adding little industry or output. The plantation way of life was set, and there was strong resistance to any change. Plantation owners thought of themselves as lords and ran their estates like English manors.

The Compromise of 1850 also entrenched sectional ideologies, so that while it squashed any current conflict, in the long term, the compromise made reconciliation impossible. Neither side would be willing to give anything up; each was furious at the other for its gains. In delaying a conflict in the present, the compromise guaranteed a war in the future.

After the compromise seemed to ease tensions, Abraham thought he would leave politics behind. He rode the circuit twice a year for ten weeks at a time. Occasionally he would fill in for Judge Davis when Davis would take off on other business. Lincoln was chosen specifically by Davis above the other lawyers because Davis thought so highly of his intelligence.

President Fillmore, once an attendee of the Rivers and Harbors convention and faithful to his roots, frequently passed bills to improve the infrastructure of the inland United States. A large railway grant was given to Illinois; both Stephen Douglas and Lincoln lobbied for the bill. Douglas, now wealthy with money from his Mississippi plantation, owned the land just south of Chicago that the railroad would run through. In February 1851, shortly after the death of Lincoln's father, the railroad was approved, and construction began. Douglas and Lincoln were usually on the same page when it came to infrastructure spending.

By now, the two had a well-established relationship, having argued many times in the statehouse against each other. When they weren't working, they would often sit at the local drugstore and tell stories to the group of lawyers assembled. They were friendly with one another, though they ended up on opposite sides more often than not. In many ways, they were mirror images of one another, both skilled orators and political dealmakers. Lincoln had a high opinion of Douglas, and many times, Douglas called him a friend. There was no animosity between the two, only respect forged from their frequent campaigns against one another; they were good friends but political foes.

The following years of Lincoln's life were full of travel, crossing the state to argue cases. Even when he was not riding the circuit, he was far from home; clients called for him from all over Illinois to represent them. His time on the circuit had earned him a reputation of honesty and intelligence. It was there that he picked up the nickname Honest Abe. Abraham was earning close to $3,000 a year from his busy law practice. His financial future was secured by a new client, the Illinois Central Railroad, which he had lobbied to create. He learned the nuances of corporate law, and the wealthy company paid him well. Mary and the children saw him very little in these years. Robert later recalled that his earliest memories of his father were of him packing his bags before a trip.

When he was home, life was happy. Mary got a chance to pamper her husband like one of her children, and he would fret if she was unwell. Their children were their happiness, and they received more joy when their fourth son was born. Thomas "Tad" Lincoln was born on April 4, 1853. Abraham noted how he wriggled like a tadpole and the name stuck. Perhaps the biggest point of contention between Mary and Abraham was their social standing. Mary frequently hosted parties and luncheons in their home, spending lavishly to impress, while her husband did not care much for appearances, happy to wear his old shirts and shabby hat. He once greeted Mary's guests in his shirtsleeves, an embarrassment Mary made sure to punish him for.

So, while Lincoln was the farthest he would ever be from politics in his adult life, this period when he was practicing law throughout Illinois and living happily in Springfield built a base from which he would reenter. A network of friends, many of whom were local and state politicians, had been formed from his time on the circuit. Clients he worked for remembered his straightforward manner, much like the people of New Salem came to know him from his time as storekeeper and mailman. Traveling around was easy as, throughout the state, his internal improvements allowed transportation to move freely. In Chicago, he remained a political celebrity: crowds in the thousands gathered to hear him speak.

The city had grown since his first visit five years earlier; thirty thousand people lived there. A high demand for new buildings and the frequent small fires meant that the city changed with every visit. The Sauganash Hotel burned down in 1851, erasing that piece of old Chicago history. The Chicago Board of Trade began in 1848, one of the first futures exchanges and a sign of a maturing city. With the completion of the Illinois-Michigan Canal, shipments of grain began to go through the city destined for world markets. Chicago had become a manufacturing center. Industry had noticed that the Great Lakes cut down on transportation costs. In this way, Chicago was geographically fortunate and the center of national infrastructure. Raw goods could be brought in easily, and manufactured goods could be shipped all over the country, though oddly enough, the city still had poor roads. For the first time in human history, the fastest transport was not the horse but the steam engine. Steam engines were put into ships first, allowing them to sail against the wind, drastically reducing travel time. Soon after, the steam locomotive was invented, and railroads began crisscrossing the nation, reducing trips that took days to mere hours. The industrial section of the city was along the north branch of the river, an area set aside for factories since Chicago first became a city. Chicago's first mayor, William Ogden, began a company there to dig up clay from the water's edge for bricks; the digging eventually created manmade Goose Island. Within fifty years, Chicago would be a leader in brick production, its blue clay bricks used throughout the country.

Cyrus McCormick, the first big industrialist to move operations to Chicago, came in 1847 and used the excellent infrastructure to get his mechanical reaper across the world. The reaper was a horse-drawn row of blades that cut wheat into neat piles. It could harvest in hours grain that used to take days. This invention revolutionized farm labor as it reduced the number of people needed for the harvest, subsequently creating a population boom in cities as former field hands looked for work. The Cyrus reaper was mass-produced in Chicago in a plant along the river; production reached four thousand a year. In 1851, the reaper was featured as an example of American mechanical ingenuity at the Crystal Palace

Exhibition in London, where McCormick's invention won first place in a grain-harvesting competition and he was admitted to the Legion of Honor. Chicago manufacturing was world renowned.

Abraham was happily removed from politics and would have remained so if the Compromise of 1850 was upheld by Congress. In 1852, Henry Clay died. Abraham's ideal statesman, the strongest voice for the West, he had founded the Whig Party to represent the West's interests and oppose Jacksonian Democrats. With his death, the Whigs lost the pin holding them together, and the party began to fall apart at the seams.

New parties began to gain steam, such as the Free-Soil Party and the Know-Nothing Party. The latter began as more of a political cult. Know-Nothings were nativists, anti-immigrant and anti-Catholic. These smaller parties would prove to be historical footnotes compared to the party that would form from them.

Abraham gave a eulogy in Springfield for the deceased Clay. In the Hall of Representatives in the state capitol building, he delivered his speech to an attentive audience. Eulogies were long public affairs, a chance for the crowd to hear the life and achievements of great people told like the stories of biblical heroes. Abraham made Henry Clay into a lion of liberty whose speeches inspired people to fight for freedom across the world. He spent time praising Clay's speaking ability and the times when he ended any threat of secession. Lincoln's speech gives insight to the qualities that he himself admired: the ability to compromise to save the center, opposition to anarchy, kindness in all things, respect for the law and a supreme power of speech. All these were traits that he himself possessed, inspiring loyalty in all those who would push him to become president.

In Washington, the death of Henry Clay set off a chain of events. The Whigs were thrashed in the election of 1852. The Whigs once again ran with a hero of the Mexican-American War, Winfield Scott, hoping his war record would win him the presidency. The Democrats ran their own war hero, Franklin Pierce. While Pierce won 43 percent of the vote, Winfield Scott only carried four states. The Democrats took the House with a forty-seat majority. The Senate was also in their hands, albeit with a one-seat majority.

With such a huge popular mandate, Senate leader Stephen Douglas got to work on a bitter issue: a railway. It was a railway meant to connect the state of California to the rest of the nation. Douglas wanted it to go through Chicago, ensuring that all the wealth of California moved through his constituency. Southern senators wanted the railway to go through their states. So Douglas, chairman of the Committee on Territories, decided to kill two birds with one stone. Any railway from Chicago to California would have to go through the Nebraska territory. Douglas, who held firm to the idea of western expansion, offered to open up the land to settlement and begin the process of statehood. This would provide the laborers and infrastructure to make the continent-spanning railway. In order to get the southern votes he needed, the new territory would be divided into two new potential states, Kansas and Nebraska. These states would be free or slave based on popular sovereignty.

Douglas's plan sparked a massive national reaction. Slave owners were delighted. They had been consigned to the land below the 36°30′parallel in the Missouri Compromise, one of Henry Clay's brilliant legal maneuvers. New slave states could not join the Union if they were above that line. However, past Texas lay the deserts of Utah and New Mexico. Plantation slavery could not exist in those climates, boxing slavery into one corner of the nation. Douglas was offering slave owners states that had been locked off, new land for them to get rich off of—and if what he wanted in return was a measly railway contract, it was no skin off their teeth.

Meanwhile, the North was outraged. Northerners had thought those lands would become free states, allowing them to gain eventual supremacy in the legislature. In their minds, Douglas had no right to repeal the Missouri Compromise. It was a betrayal of his state and of his friend Henry Clay. What infuriated the North even further was that it did not have the means in Congress to oppose the bill: there just weren't enough Whigs in office. Democrats in the North deserted the party structure, calling themselves Anti-Nebraska Democrats. They were not the only new movement opposed to Douglas and his bill.

In Ripon, Wisconsin, former Whigs and Anti-Nebraska Democrats joined together to form a new party. Sources differ on who gave the party its name—both Horace Greely and Joseph Medill claim to have christened it—but the newly formed Republican Party took the North by storm. It campaigned under a big tent, aiming at bringing all the small northern parties into the fold. Its slogan was "Free Soil, Free Trade, Free Men." It did not seek to end slavery but rather to contain it under the Missouri Compromise line to the north and east of New Mexico and Utah. It sought to open the land west for settlement, to ensure that free men would not have to compete against plantation owners. And it wanted railways and infrastructure to build a new, modern America. The Fugitive Slave Law would be repealed, so that citizens who objected to slavery were not legally required to perpetuate it.

Quickly flocking to the banner were big business interests and industrialists; abolitionists who wanted the total death of slavery, not just its containment; and immigrants attracted by the prospect of land. The Know-Nothings joined up later as the Republicans came to represent all northern interests. There were a great number of parties in the North during the tumultuous fifties, and there was never a guarantee that any of them could become a national political force. Two main factors would contribute to the Republican Party's rise. Firstly, the wealth and power of the industrialist members was allied with the vast numbers of European immigrants who believed in the Republican Free-Soil message. Secondly, the Democrats were fracturing over the Kansas-Nebraska Act. As Lincoln described in his campaign strategy in later years, it was to be a three-way fight. The Republicans would not go out of their way to pick up Anti-Nebraska Democrats—they would welcome all those who wanted to join—but they quite liked the idea of a political force that would eternally split the vote of the Democrats. Their aim was not to be an offshoot of either side but rather to offer a third solution.

Canadian-born Joseph Medill had come to the United States as a young man and passed the Ohio bar when he was twenty-three. He worked odd jobs but eventually got into newspaper publishing, starting his own paper in Cleveland. Meanwhile, the *Chicago Tribune* began in 1847. It was mainly antislavery, but in the years following the Compromise of 1850, it lost most of its readers and became a Know-Nothing paper. Part owner Dr. Charles Ray asked Medill to come and take over as editor. Medill asked his mentor Horace Greeley what he thought. Greeley encouraged him to go; some contemporaries say that his famous advice, "Go West, young man, and grow up with the country," was given to Medill. Medill came to Chicago in 1854 and quickly turned the *Tribune* around. The paper returned to an antislavery platform and became the Republican organ of Chicago. Like Abraham, the *Tribune* experienced a revival in the wake of the Kansas-Nebraska Act. Within three years, it was the most widely read paper in Illinois. Medill first met Lincoln in the *Tribune* offices on one of his visits to Chicago, when Lincoln went to buy a yearly subscription. While Lincoln was not yet a Republican, he and Medill shared similar views. Over the years, Lincoln would write a number of articles for the paper.

Chicago would quickly become a Republican bastion; the *Tribune* quickly became its voice. In previous elections, while Illinois went to Douglas and his brand of Jacksonian Democrat, Chicago remained loyal to Free-Soil; slavery was a big issue to Chicagoans. Despite Douglas adopting the city as his own, Chicago did not support him. There was a selfishness mixed in with antislavery ideals; many worried that they would not be able to compete against slave owners in an open market. Immigrant day laborers stood to lose work when faced with competition from slave labor. Selfish interests coincided with abolitionists like John Brown in the same party.

The 1850s saw Chicago become the fastest-growing city in the world, a title it would hold for three decades. It was an industrial city; dark smoke clouds belched into the sky as the industrial goods the United States needed rolled off the lines. It was a dirty city, a swampy city, but as it grew, Chicagoans grew wealthy, just in time for the arrival of the first Chicago merchant prince. While Cyrus McCormick was the city's first industrialist, a millionaire from his short time in Chicago, Potter Palmer brought style to the city. Palmer was born in New York and worked in dry goods stores. At twenty-six, he decided to try his luck in the boomtown. He opened Potter Palmer and Company on Lake Street to instant success. Palmer's products were high quality and at the cutting edge of fashion. One of the main factors of his success was that he marketed to women, whom he knew did the shopping for most households. His store offered the first money-back guarantee, taking back anything they sold, no questions asked. Palmer invented the window display, placing clearly priced clothes in large windows so Chicagoans could compare prices and inspect each product before buying. Shelves were purposely understocked to make certain items seem popular. Palmer was the first in and the last out each day, personally walking the aisles assisting customers. When it came to wholesale, Palmer was again ahead of the competition; his agents created a vast network of buyers throughout the Midwest. Competitors scoffed at his ideas, but Palmer was a millionaire within two years, and soon, others were copying his model.

Merchants became a fixture of the city. One of the largest rivals of Palmer was John V. Farwell. He had been living in Chicago since the 1840s, arriving with $3.50 and a Bible in his pocket. He worked for various dry goods stores before starting his own, John Farwell and Company. The company did most of its business in wholesaling, competing head-to-head with Palmer in small Midwest stores, but in retail they had only a small department. Farwell had a warehouse in the industrial part of the city, along the north branch of the river. He was a noted philanthropist, bringing the YMCA to Chicago and helping set up the Moody Bible Church. Shortly after Palmer came the Honoré family from Louisville, Kentucky. H.H. Honoré set up his dry goods store on Pearl Street and was quickly admitted to the Chicago elite. He had two daughters, Bertha and Ida, who were educated at the Dearborn Academy. Instead of becoming a rival, Honoré was close friends with Palmer. When the Honoré daughters visited his shop, Palmer waited on them himself.

In late 1854, Abraham campaigned for anti-Douglas candidates, giving a number of speeches on Douglas's betrayal of the Missouri Compromise. He had been happy to stay out of politics and practice law, but Douglas's bold bill went too far. Abraham and his friends campaigned to keep the state from falling into Douglas's hands. Abraham would no longer remain silent, launching a campaign for a seat in the state legislature. He was still a Whig, holding to the hope that the party might once again lead at the forefront of national politics. The Kansas-Nebraska debate might just be what his party needed to come back; after all, it was what he had needed to get back into politics. He declined an offer to join the Republicans, who were too extreme, in his view. Abraham returned triumphantly to the halls of the Illinois legislature for the first time since 1842. The election of 1854 brought thirty-seven Republicans to Congress and was also the last time a third party would have sway in the government, as fifty Know-Nothings sat with them. In Illinois, no party had a majority in the legislature, but the members opposing the Kansas-Nebraska Act outnumbered their opponents by thirteen. It was time for the legislature to pick a senator, and Lincoln hoped it would be him.

Before the Seventeenth Amendment required senators to be elected by direct popular vote, the state legislatures would decide the process. Lincoln had his friends work the newly elected legislature to pick him. They worked hard at it, cornering representatives in the halls and convincing them to vote his way. Lincoln was still running as a Whig and could avoid the radicalism that hung around the new Republicans. The first ballot showed just how good Lincoln's men had been. He was in the lead with forty-four votes. Shields, the man he had almost fought a duel with, came in second as the choice of the Douglas Democrats. Lyman Trumbull, an Anti-Nebraska Democrat, was in third. There were a small number of other candidates. Had the five voters for Trumbull switched to Lincoln, he would have gone to the Senate in 1855. Both candidates were Anti-Nebraska, and switching from Trumbull to Lincoln should have been no problem at all, but Trumbull's backers refused to switch, stubbornly following the lead of one Norman B. Judd. A well-groomed Chicago lawyer, Judd loved politics, having served in public office since he was twenty-two. By the seventh vote, the Douglas supporters had switched from Shields to Governor Joel Matteson, and Lincoln was down to only seventeen votes. On the tenth ballot, Lincoln knew that he couldn't win. He told his supporters to vote for Trumbull, which put Trumbull over the top. A dejected Abraham declined to take his seat in the state legislature.

If Lincoln felt any bitterness toward the Trumbull holdouts, he did not show it. The many Anti-Nebraska representatives there would shortly join the Republican Party and become the most loyal of Lincoln's men. Trumbull would become coauthor of the Thirteenth Amendment, the main goal of Lincoln's Reconstruction policy. One of those present would nominate Lincoln for vice president. Nearly all of those who were Anti-Nebraska at that time backed Lincoln for Senate when he ran against Douglas four years later. Judd holds a special place among all these new allies: he was the man who made Lincoln president.

The fact that, in the future, their fidelity to Abraham would preserve the Union did not earn these men friends among his current backers, who felt betrayed. Lincoln's former law partner Stephen Logan was furious at what had happened. Judge David Davis didn't trust Judd, and William Herndon would not forgive him for blocking Lincoln from the Senate. Mary Lincoln never again spoke to Trumbull's wife, who had been a bridesmaid at her wedding; she could not forgive the theft of her husband's seat.

After this disappointment, Lincoln returned to his law practice. Unlike before, he would not ignore politics while he traveled. He was making connections and building friendships across Illinois: a network of people he could rely on, grassroots, gathering supporters on a local level. Few disliked him or remembered his disastrous time in Congress; even his frequent opponent Douglas had nothing but a glowing opinion of him.

In July 1855, Lincoln came to Chicago, arguing in front of the district court. He would remain there another sixteen days, occasionally having tea with the opposing council. With every visit, Lincoln found Republicans in increasing numbers. While in Chicago, Abraham had been hired for a patent case. Cyrus McCormick was suing one John Manny from Rockford, Illinois. Manny had recently developed a reaper to compete with McCormick's, which outsold his design. Well known for litigiousness, McCormick was out for blood. Out-of-town lawyers want local knowledge, and Abraham had been hired by the defense based on glowing recommendations. The lawyers he would work for were George Harding and Edwin M. Stanton; the latter objected to Lincoln's involvement, saying, "Where did that long-armed baboon come from?" The trial, originally to take place in Chicago, was moved to Cincinnati, and Lincoln was no longer needed, but he was not told so. He traveled to Ohio nonetheless, taking one of his boys with him. Lincoln played almost no part in the trial, but once again, his defeat would turn to victory down the road. Stanton, despite his poor first impression of Lincoln, would later become his secretary of war. It was Lincoln's nature to turn opponents into friends.

The rest of 1855, Abraham worked a great number of cases, but not in Chicago. The city at the time was reaching one hundred thousand inhabitants and had become the railway hub for all the United States. It had a brand-new university, built on land donated by Senator Douglas, next to his home. Critics said he was trying to raise the value of the land he kept, but Douglas had always been a firm believer in the people, his character genuine. He paid critics no mind. Though he was burned in effigy across the North, Douglas remained in the bastion of antislavery feeling. Despite being well liked in the southern parts of the state, he saw a future in Chicago. His wife died in 1853, and in 1856, he married Adele Cutts, grandniece of Dolley Madison. A Jacksonian Democrat, Douglas believed the people were a sovereign force and it was up to them to decide the fate of the nation. Let the people of a state decide the rules of that state. But his high-minded ideals were tarnished by reality.

Kansas became a war zone. Slave owners in Missouri would sneak across state lines to vote and intimidate free state advocates. They burned a hotel and smashed two printing presses. The outraged North had its own radical, John Brown. He had an organized militia numbering in the hundreds that would attack proslavery gangs. In all, close to one hundred were killed and more wounded, thousands of dollars of property destroyed. Rival legislatures sent Congress different constitutions for the state, usually illegally.

Anti-Nebraska sentiment helped to fuel the Republican Party. In May 1856, the vast array of Douglas opponents met in Bloomington, Illinois, to decide on a state ticket. Now known as the first Illinois State Republican Convention, it was more a gathering of the minor parties willing to hear out the Republican platform. Chicago Republicans sent Judd. There were also newspaper men, most notably Joseph Medill. Abraham had been nervous coming to such a convention. He believed that the Republicans were a group of abolitionist radicals and continued to cling to the Whigs. Watching as the delegates came in, Lincoln said of Judd's arrival, "Judd is here, and he's a trimmer." Judd's presence eased his fears, as Lincoln had come to know him as a moderate voice, and helped Lincoln as he listened to the Republican platform.

Lincoln's own speech at the convention would be one of his most famous, though not one word of it was ever written down. In his so-called lost speech, he spoke so captivatingly that none of the dozens of reporters present wrote down his words. Those present were enthralled by the conviction with which he denounced the Kansas-Nebraska bill. Medill wrote that Lincoln started off "soft and then built to a storm." When the time came to break apart, the crowd leaving the convention was Republican.

A month later, while arguing a case, Lincoln was shown a Chicago newspaper covering the first Republican convention in Philadelphia: he had won 110 votes for vice president on the national ticket. Clearly, he had made a name for himself. Now solidly a Republican, Lincoln campaigned for the party in the election of 1856. He toured much of western Illinois in that campaign, visiting cities such as Galena, Dixon and Sterling. In Galena, a large city in the northwestern corner of the state, he gave a speech from the balcony of the DeSoto Hotel, which still stands today. His audience consisted mainly of well-to-do ladies, who listened earnestly to his speech. Little is known of what he said there, but the newspapers wrote that it was well received. Lincoln also spoke in Dixon that year, a town he passed through frequently, always staying in the same room of the Nachusa House hotel. He stayed at the Manahan House in Sterling, a building that stands today as a museum. While Buchanan, a Democrat, won the presidency, the Republican Party proved that it had a strong base of support by winning 30 percent of the vote. The North had its party.

A sign of Lincoln's growing popularity in Illinois, the people of the Third District had invited him to speak at a rally for the Republican candidate. He had hoped for his friend Leonard Swett to be the nominee, but instead, a man named Owen Lovejoy won. Lincoln thought about canceling but went to boost his profile. Arriving by train in Tiskilwa, he stayed the night at the Utopia Hotel before attending "probably the largest meeting ever held in the county" in Princeton. Owen Lovejoy was an ardent abolitionist whose brother had been killed by a proslavery mob. When in Congress and accused of aiding runaway slaves, he said, "Proclaim it upon the house-tops!…Owen Lovejoy lives at Princeton Illinois, three-quarters of a mile east of the village, and he aids every fugitive that comes to his door and asks it." Lovejoy was the sort of abolitionist radical that Lincoln had thought the Republican Party was made of. While disappointed with the choice of Lovejoy, Lincoln gave a calm and measured speech to the crowd, urging them to vote against those who would betray the free states. Lovejoy would win his election and become one of the staunchest supporters of Lincoln and his presidency. The choice of Lincoln for a speaker would have seemed strange to someone coming to the event. He was not well known in Princeton; it was only in the corridor between Springfield and Chicago that he was recognized as a speaker. The man who would host Lincoln for dinner, Stephen Paddock, wrote later that fewer than one hundred people recognized him; all eyes were focused on their hometown hero Lovejoy. Yet Lincoln's invitation to speak was recognition of his place within the political scene of Illinois. No matter whom he gave his speeches to, he was praised for speaking in plain and honest language, never changing his position for political expedience. After his speech in Princeton, Lincoln had a daguerreotype taken of him, one crisp and clear that showed an untidy, travel-worn but still young Lincoln, not yet burdened with the weight of the coming war.

The national political landscape was not all that was changing. Returning from a stint on the circuit, Abraham found that his home had a second story all of a sudden. Mary, with her inheritance and the help of James Gourley, had procured the contractors Hannan & Ragsdale to give her family of five more room. Not recognizing his little cottage turned into a two-story home, he reportedly asked a passerby on which street the attorney Lincoln lived. The cost for such a job was approximately $1,300. That the Lincoln family could afford the renovation shows that the last few years had been good to them.

Whenever Lincoln returned, his happy family was waiting for him. Robert was more of a Todd than a Lincoln, not as close to his father as he was to his mother. For much of his childhood, his father was traveling. William was already a thoughtful child, and Tad spent his time running around. Abraham did not send his younger two children to school. An indulgent father, he wanted to be everything to his sons that his father was not to him. He would not raise his voice or discipline them when they were causing trouble, letting them crawl all over him when he was meeting with guests. When Mary scolded the children, Abraham would always be there to calm her down and let the kids off the hook. They played with the neighboring Gourley children frequently.

Abraham went to Chicago briefly in July to campaign for the presidential election. The Republican candidate, John Fremont, was the first ever to run for the party. Lincoln had come close to being his running mate but had lost the nomination in the end. Once again, though Illinois went to the Democrats under Buchanan, Chicago went to the Republicans. The election proved that the young party was on the national stage, but if they wanted to win the presidency, they needed a candidate that could unite the northern states.

Lincoln went to Chicago twice at the end of 1856, once passing through and once on a court case. When in Chicago, Lincoln almost always stayed

The Lincoln home in Springfield as it stands today. It was the only home Abraham ever owned and where the children grew up. During the presidency it was rented out, and after the assassination it was turned into a museum by the renter. Returning was too painful for Mary; instead, the family settled in Chicago. *Collection of John Toman.*

at Ida Couch's Tremont House Hotel. A massive hotel with close to three hundred rooms, the Tremont was home to all visiting politicians. A visitor called it "the mecca in those days; and thither, all political pilgrims came." The Tremont boasted fine food and elegant dining halls and had been a part of Chicago, in one building or another, since 1833. At the end of 1856, as he prepared to go home to Springfield, Lincoln delivered a joking toast at a banquet for three hundred Republican politicians, one that would turn into a grave prophesy of the future. "The Union," he toasted, "the North shall maintain it—the South shall not depart therefrom."

Chapter 4

THE FAVORITE SON

In January 1856, Lincoln argued the case of the Illinois Central Railroad before the state supreme court. He had started working for them in 1853 and would be lead council on a total of eleven cases. Mclean County wanted to tax the company's property, but the charter given by the state had exempted the company from tax in return for a percentage of its profits. It was the third time this particular case was heard in court. The opposing council was John Stuart and Steven Logan, both Lincoln's former law partners. In this third trial, the verdict was unanimous in the company's favor. He presented the company with a bill for an unheard-of $5,000. Though legal bills of that size were not uncommon in New York, this was the largest legal bill yet in the frontier states. Illinois Central was in a tough position: the fee was exorbitant, but Lincoln's services were indispensable. So the company presented a compromise. Lincoln sued them, submitting the opinions of seven lawyers, each stating that the $5,000 was fair for the work he had done. The Illinois Central Railroad sent no representative; the verdict was given to Lincoln by default. Among the seven lawyers was Steven Logan, who had just lost to him in this very case, and Norman Judd, along with two other lawyers from Chicago. Lincoln received the $4,800 that was still unpaid after the retainer. This was the largest paycheck that he ever received prior to becoming president.

Unsure of whether or not he still worked for Illinois Central due to his suit against them, Lincoln went to their offices in Chicago to find out in early 1857. The company happily kept him on, even giving him cases while he sued them. While in Chicago, he sat for his first photograph with Alexander Hesler, a Chicago-based photographer whose photos track Lincoln's rise to prominence. Lincoln had photos of himself taken frequently, more so than most people of the day. This was not a vanity. The abundant pictures were of political use, helpful for publicity, so that supporters knew his face and felt an attachment to him. Abraham certainly did not think himself handsome. When an opponent called him two-faced, he responded "If I had two faces, why would I be wearing this one?" Later, when he was president, an official tendered his resignation, and Abraham replied, "All right, Addison, I accept your resignation but nothing can compensate me for the loss of you, for when you retire I will be the ugliest man left in the employ of the Government." His often self-deprecating humor helped set people at ease and make them feel in on the joke, though no record can say what Addison thought about it.

On the last day of Lincoln's stay, he was invited to give a speech at Metropolitan Hall on the corner of LaSalle and Randolph Streets. Here, Republicans were deciding their ticket for local elections. It was one of the few occasions when Lincoln gave an unscheduled speech. Normally when he came to Chicago to work, there was always someone who wanted him to speak on one topic or another. Unscheduled speeches were a distraction he tried to avoid. When working an important case, he would avoid the Tremont because it was too easy for the crowds to find him there. At these times, he would stay in the homes of friends. But since this visit was not for a case, he gladly gave a speech. The Chicago Republicans were split over supporting John Wentworth. Lincoln urged them to hold true to their party and avoid factionalism; by securing Chicago for the Republicans, they could secure the state. He was cheered on by an adoring crowd; support for Lincoln was stronger than ever in Chicago. This sentiment was aided in no small part by Joseph Medill and his newspaper.

Medill had the largest newspaper by subscription in the West and was not afraid to use it. He constantly attacked Stephen Douglas and his paper, the *Chicago Times*, as well as the rival *Chicago Democrat*, owned by John Wentworth. Since his first meeting with Lincoln, Medill was a supporter. Whenever Lincoln gave a speech, there was a *Tribune* reporter in the crowd taking notes. His paper never said a bad word about Lincoln.

In the mayoral election of 1857, the first Republican mayor was elected: Long John Wentworth. He had served as Chicago's congressman four times as a Democrat, but he broke with Douglas over the Kansas-Nebraska Act, joining the Republican Party around the same time as Lincoln. Wentworth continued to own and operate the *Chicago Democrat* as a Republican, and there was no love lost between him and Medill. Part of the animosity was from the close friendship between Medill and Norman B. Judd, whom Wentworth hated. Another reason was Medill's ideological purity; he was suspicious of Wentworth's commitment to the party.

Wentworth's time as mayor gave Medill plenty of ammo: he was one of the more memorable characters to hold the position, using the power of his office as he saw fit. The giant Vermont native liked to dress well, was full of bluster and was not afraid to speak his mind. The red-haired mayor rode a white horse and swore like a sailor. He did do good things for the city. An advocate of public schools, he had the city's first brick schoolhouse built. But his year in office was also marked by gaffes. When he learned a lawyer by the name of Charles Cameron was visiting his client in prison, he went there, grabbed Cameron by his lapels and threw him out of the building. Wentworth was ordered to appear in court for his behavior but refused to appear and was made to pay $225 to Cameron. Perhaps the most famous moment of his term was his raid on the Sands. The Chicago River did not go straight into Lake Michigan in those days but turned right before flowing into the lake, creating a large sandbar. As Chicago grew, its seedier side set up on the sandbar. A red-light district of brothels and gambling dens covered the narrow strip of land, known as the Sands. Wentworth wanted to remove the eyesore and so personally led a police raid on it. They moved in, sweeping from one side of the Sands to the other, pulling down buildings as they went. At some point, a fire broke out that burned the Sands to the ground. Wentworth congratulated himself for a job well done, but Medill was unimpressed.

Small fires were a common occurrence in Chicago. The largest fire Chicago had seen was in October 1857, when a lantern was knocked over in a brothel beside the Illinois Central Railroad depot at the mouth of the river. The fire grew out of control quickly and burned along the waterfront. Twenty-three people died, and the flames caused $800,000 of property damage. Among the dead were a number of firefighters. Afterward, Mayor Wentworth raised thousands of dollars to better equip the volunteer Chicago Fire Department; in gratitude, their first steam engine was named after him.

Abraham would come to Chicago three more times in 1857. Once was in late May, though it was a trip so short that little is known of what he did. The other two times were to defend the Railroad Bridge Company against powerful steamboat interests based in St. Louis. Chicago and St. Louis were rivals. St. Louis was the major grain depot of the nation, and Chicago was an up-and-coming city hoping to take that title, so the two

The Graceland tomb of fireman John Dickey, who was killed in the fire of 1857, the most devastating fire Chicago had known up to that point. The disaster proved that the volunteer fire department was not equipped to handle large fires. Mayor "Long" John Wentworth gave money to better outfit them. *Christopher Phillips.*

cities vied for control of shipping. The steamer *Effie Afton* had collided with the first railroad bridge over the Mississippi. Hoping to protect their control of Mississippi transportation and keep railroads from taking their business, the owners sued. Lincoln was hired for the defense, having become an expert in railway law through working for railroad companies the last four years. The case was heard in Chicago. Lincoln surveyed the site of the accident himself, taking care to note the currents. His argument was that as the bridge was stationary, the captain would have to prove the ship was piloted exceptionally well in order to lay any burden on the railway. While in Chicago for the initial hearings, Abraham joined a group of Republican politicians at the Tremont: O.M. Hatch, Jesse DuBois, Lyman Trumbull and others. The nature of the Tremont allowed Abraham to network, building a group of friends with his storytelling and jokes. The next day, he went with some of these to see a famous comedy of the time, *The Toodles*, starring William Burton. Abraham loved theater, and Chicago was where he could see the best there was.

Lincoln's stay at the Tremont with the prominent figures of the Republican Party helped him understand the political lay of the land. The party was preparing to turn Douglas out of his seat, punishment for betraying the North. Douglas, in the meantime, had split with President Buchanan over a fraudulent state constitution from Kansas, further dividing the strength of the Democrats. If they were ever to win the state, the time was fast approaching.

Returning to Chicago in September to finish the *Effie Afton* case, Lincoln would be supported in the courtroom by Norman Judd and Joseph Knox. Judd was now an important member of the Illinois Republican scene and a power broker, although David Davis and Wentworth still did not trust him. The case resulted in a hung jury, and the judge dismissed the case. The future of railroad construction west had been saved, guaranteeing Chicago's key place in American infrastructure.

Judd, Medill, Wentworth and Davis were not yet set on Lincoln for president in 1857, and while they were all his good friends, they did not get along with one another. Medill was a newspaper mogul who would write someone off for lack of Republican purity, Judd was a hotshot lawyer—and former Democrat—who liked to wheel and deal, Wentworth was too abrasive to get along with most people and Judge Davis did not trust the others.

With depositions every day, Abraham's stay that September would be his longest in Chicago, a total of twenty-four days with the case taking up all his time. He had previously been offered a job at a law firm in Chicago, but he had declined, fearing that if he moved his family into the city, he would be exposing them to diseases. The sanitary movement was just beginning, but still, in most cities, waste lay in the streets, and diseases like tuberculosis and influenza were rampant. More people died in cities than were born in them.

At the end of Lincoln's extended stay in Chicago, he returned home. Springfield had grown, too, since he had first come there in 1837. There were close to two thousand people when he first arrived, and now the city had around nine thousand residents. Unlike Chicago, whose growth came from industry and waterways, Springfield had grown because it had become the state capital. Lincoln could be proud of what his city had become in such a short time; as the head of the Long Nine, he was almost singlehandedly responsible for moving the capital to Springfield.

Abraham did not stay at home for long, returning to Chicago for a case set to start the first of December. His traveling was hard on the children, especially Robert, who was seven years older than Willie. Whereas Willie and Tad were running around the neighborhood having fun and causing trouble, Robert was more serious. He helped his mother raise his siblings, dressed well and got good grades in school. The wildness of Willie and Tad exasperated Robert, and he tried to tame them, but he was a loving big brother.

Both Robert and Tad were mama's boys, but Willie was Abraham in miniature. Thoughtful and compassionate, he was the only one who could calm down Tad when he was upset. Willie loved to learn. He had a mature intellect for his age that would only grow with time. The younger sons attended a grammar school, but Tad did not stay there long. He hated schooling; he had a strong lisp that no one outside the family could understand and was teased for it. Abraham did not care that his youngest son was not attending school; he refused to discipline the boys. He defended them when Mary scolded them; he let them pinch money for sweets from him. Unlike when Robert was young, railroads allowed Abraham to come home on the weekends, regardless of where he was working in Illinois. The Illinois Central Railroad joined the state's capital to all its far-flung corners.

The year 1858 was one of great political significance for Abraham and the Republican Party at large. Stephen Douglas's senate seat was up for reelection, and throughout Illinois, Republicans were thinking of one thing: payback. It was four years since Douglas had sold Free-Soil for votes in the Senate, and those who were opposed to it finally had enough backing to knock him off his seat. Additional fuel was the Supreme Court ruling a year earlier on the Dred Scott case. The court, led by Chief Justice Roger Taney, gave a ruling far beyond its judicial power in perhaps the most despicable verdict in American history. The slave Dred Scott argued that since his owner had taken him into a free state, by the laws of that state, he was free. Taney, hoping to end the issue of slavery once and for all, declared not only that Scott was still a slave but also that banning slavery state by state was unconstitutional and that no person whose ancestors were brought to America in bondage could ever become an American citizen, effectively denying citizenship to all people of African descent.

The Dred Scott case galvanized the North, granting the Republican Party legions of new members as they deserted other parties en masse. It was with these new voters that the Illinois Republicans planned to challenge Douglas. Lincoln went to Chicago in February 1858 to meet with Judd.

They were planning to make Abraham the Republican pick for Senate. Judd was confident in Lincoln's chances; he had been to Washington just a short time earlier and had met with Douglas, whom he found "dead, gloomy, miserable—knew that he was lost." He was confident in a Republican victory come November.

In April, the Democratic State Convention chose Douglas as their man once again. Around the same time, Lincoln sent Herndon up to Chicago to talk with the party chiefs on strategy. Herndon was a lawyer in his own right but was happy to run errands for him. All Lincoln's years of networking and planning had finally placed him in a strong position, so that on June 16, the Republican State Convention in Springfield passed the resolution: "Resolved: that Abraham Lincoln is the first and only choice of the Republicans of Illinois for the United States Senate, as a successor of Stephen Douglas." Abraham's acceptance speech gave the famous line: "A house divided against itself, cannot stand." Medill's *Tribune* published the speech, and it was read nationwide. In slave states, it was denounced as dangerous radicalism. Northern Republicans welcomed the speech as a well-reasoned response to encroaching slave interests. National attention was drawn to the Senate race, and it would remain fixed there as the Lincoln-Douglas debates got underway.

The first shots were fired early. The Douglas-owned paper the *Chicago Times* attacked Abraham for refusing to vote for the troops' supplies during the Mexican-American War, which was true—Abraham had wanted to pull the United States out of that war. Lincoln wrote a rebuttal that Medill printed in his paper, a denial of his opposition to the war. Lincoln was facing a well-entrenched Douglas with a poor record in national politics and a new party; he had to win several Douglas strongholds in order to win the seat. It was Medill who suggested that Lincoln and Douglas have debates, confident in his man's ability to win a war of words. Lincoln was the best debater the Republicans had in the western states, comparable to the great eastern Seward. With the biggest paper in Illinois on his side, he began the fight.

On July 9, Abraham Lincoln was in Chicago for the third time that year (having come in March for a trial), arriving the same day as Senator Douglas. Both stayed at the Tremont Hotel that night, and Douglas spoke to the crowd gathered outside. From the balcony, he spoke for over an hour to a crowd thirty thousand strong. Lincoln was in the crowd, listening to the speech. He would have heard himself referred to as a "kind, amiable, high-minded gentleman, a good citizen and an honorable opponent." The next day, Lincoln gave his own speech from that balcony. The crowd was slightly smaller but was far more enthusiastic, according to the *Tribune*. In his speech, Lincoln admitted that he thought slavery was wrong on moral grounds and that he believed the Dred Scott decision must be reversed to allow people of African descent citizenship, but he was not going to end slavery. He attacked Douglas for blowing things out of proportion and using fear to protect his place in the Senate.

Lincoln would stay in Chicago a couple of days longer, having tea with some friends and strategizing his campaign. He would return to Chicago on the twenty-first of July to talk with party leaders. On the final day of his stay in Chicago, he formally challenged Douglas to a series of debates all around Illinois, one in each of its congressional districts. Since they had already given speeches in Chicago and Springfield within a day of each other, they would not debate there. In the other districts, first one candidate would speak for an hour, then his opponent would speak for an hour and a half, then finally the first speaker would give a half-hour rebuttal. Douglas would be the first speaker in four debates, as he was the incumbent.

The speeches gained national attention; people from neighboring states would come and listen. Newspapers printed full transcripts of the debates across the nation, editing the transcript of their preferred candidate and leaving their opponent's speech as it was written down by reporters, full of spelling errors. Medill, as an unofficial campaign manager, worked with Lincoln on his speeches and spent the *Tribune*'s resources promoting him. Medill knew the power of newspapers to form public opinion, and as owner of the largest paper in the state, Medill pulled no punches. He organized special train rates for Chicagoans to get to these debates and support Lincoln.

At the debate in Freeport, Illinois, Lincoln asked Douglas a series of questions on his support of slavery—one of which, crucially, was how Douglas's love for popular sovereignty would hold up in the wake of the Dred Scott case, which had declared that all territories were open to slavery. Douglas answered that the principle of popular sovereignty was still in effect, that slaves could be moved into the territories but that should the state decide to be a free state, slavery would be banned. Douglas gained support throughout Illinois for his stance, known as the Freeport Doctrine, but given the national nature of the campaign, Southern Democrats were outraged at his defiance of the Supreme Court; Douglas was no longer trusted in the South. This question posed by Lincoln killed any chance Douglas had of becoming president.

The debates made Lincoln famous throughout the country. To Republicans, he was a hero taking on the dangerous Douglas. Though Horace Greeley supported Douglas, he nevertheless gave Lincoln glowing coverage in his paper. In the election, Lincoln won more than half the popular vote. As the districts had been gerrymandered by the Democrats, the state legislature was theirs with a comfortable ten-seat majority, but all five votes from Chicago and Cook County were for Lincoln. Douglas had defended his seat, and Lincoln's senatorial dreams were once again stopped on the floor of the state capitol.

While the debates won the seat for Douglas and lost him the presidency, it was the reverse for Lincoln. It is quite probable that without the national attention the debates received, he would not have become president. Lincoln and Douglas were household names. Afterward, Lincoln published the full text of the debates; his book sold sixteen thousand copies. While Lincoln was riding high after his defeat, many of those who had supported him found fault once again with Judd. There were complaints made about Judd's wasting party funds by promoting his and Trumbull's future campaigns. Lincoln never accused him, but David Davis was outraged, and Herndon had all his suspicions confirmed. They could not trust Judd. Medill was disappointed with the loss but, in an interview with Douglas, became convinced that Douglas would join the Republican Party by 1860 and took heart. Medill wrote to Salmon Chase of Ohio to let him know the *Tribune* supported his upcoming presidential campaign.

So it seemed that the lost election drove Lincoln's three key supporters away. Davis was dejected, Judd was looking at Trumbull and Medill was courting Ohio for the next Republican president. Lincoln seems to have been the only one who believed he had a future in elected office. The attention his campaign received meant that he had offers to give speeches in other states, raising his profile ever further.

Shortly after his defeat, Lincoln returned to Chicago for yet another trial. While this was a routine visit for him, it was a special visit for someone else. George Pullman was a young engineer who came to Chicago in order to raise the Matterson House six feet above ground. He had grown up on the banks of the Erie Canal; his father was an inventor who had helped widen the canal. Chicago was built in a swamp, and the city planned to install a complete sewer system. In order to do so, the city had to be raised about six feet. Pullman and his partners would lift building after building with hydraulic jacks; the building would then have a new foundation built underneath. A raising would take several days, with hundreds of men slowly cranking their hydraulic jacks until the building reached the desired height. There were no reports of damage to any of the buildings that Pullman worked on. He became such an expert that his company could raise an entire city block

Stephen Douglas was known as the Little Giant for his small stature and dominant political influence. When he lived in Springfield, he often spent time telling stories with Abraham Lincoln and other lawyers at Speed's general store. *Library of Congress, LC-USZ62-1754.*

or entire row of homes at a time, as crowds watched in awe. The process was slow, so businesses being lifted continued to operate normally. After the Matterson House was lifted, a surprised guest noted that the steps seemed steeper than when he checked in. If Abraham was in town when the lifting began, it is a certainty that he would have watched. He loved mechanical engineering, and the chance to see large buildings lifted with nothing more than manpower and ingenuity was not something he would pass up.

Chicago was becoming increasingly metropolitan. The railroads had connected it to the vast resources of the nation, allowing it to build technological wonders that would have been all but impossible a few years earlier. The city had only recently celebrated its twentieth year, and one hundred thousand people lived there. Chicago had experienced a number of disease outbreaks, but the Raising of Chicago greatly improved its health. Its stores were the equal of New York's, and its merchants were riding high. John Farwell brought on the young and talented Marshall Field and Levi Leiter as partners.

While Chicago had its distinct Republican factions, they were all united behind Abraham. He was not universally loved, but he was certainly the most recognizable and popular Republican in Illinois after his debates with Douglas. It did not hurt to have the *Tribune* backing him. His home in Springfield and work in Chicago gave him recognition in the political and economic centers of the state. By 1858, Lincoln was fully committed to politics, and in the wake of his defeat to Douglas, he began to sound out future campaigns with Judd.

Judd's love of politics and the fact that he knew every key politician in the state made him the ideal sounding board for Lincoln. In 1859, Abraham bought a small Springfield German-language paper called the *Illinois Staat-Anzeiger* for $400. In America, German was the most spoken language after English, especially in the Midwest, where many Germans, Dutch and Polish immigrants came. Lincoln's involvement with the newspaper was kept a secret; only he, the editor, his banker and one trusted colleague knew. Abraham did not interfere with the daily running of the paper but asked that occasional editorials in his favor be published to gain favor with the substantial German voting bloc. German immigrants were staunch Republicans and, if won over, could be a decisive factor in future campaigns.

Lincoln returned home from Chicago upon hearing that Tad was sick. By the time he returned, Tad was healthy again. He had already lost one child to disease while he was away, so it must have been a great relief for him to return to a healthy household. Such a sudden journey would not have been possible earlier, but with the Illinois Central Railway, he was able to come home at short notice. The train ride from Chicago to Springfield took only a few hours, enabling Abraham to come home on weekends.

On June 3, Abraham came to Chicago with his son Willie. It is unclear why he came to Chicago at this time, as he was defending a client in court in Springfield, losing the case by default when he did not appear. They stayed at the Tremont. Willie wrote to a friend how much he loved the city: "This town is a very beautiful place. Me and father have a nice little room to ourselves. We have two little pitchers on a washstand. The smallest one for me the largest one for father. We have two little towels on a top of both pitchers. The smallest one for me, the largest one for father. Me and father had gone to two theaters the other night." Abraham loved the theaters, and the opportunity to take his son to see the best shows in the state must have been a special one for the pair.

Abraham and Willie returned to Chicago on July 19 with the whole family. They were accompanied by friends and cousins from Springfield. The trip was part of the duties of the auditor of public accounts to assess how much the Illinois Central Railroad owed the state, and Lincoln helped with the job. Like Willie, the Lincoln family loved the big city—Mary especially liked shopping at the metropolitan stores, such as that of Potter Palmer—and they all loved the theaters. Had Abraham moved his family to Chicago, no one would have complained. The next months were busy for him, traveling the country on a public speaking tour, trying to raise his profile in key Republican strongholds.

In late September 1859, Abraham went to Milwaukee, passing through Chicago on the way. He had been invited to deliver the annual address at the Wisconsin State Fair. The *Chicago Tribune* printed his speech in full. It was less fiery than others; Abraham praised the advancement of technology (much of which was manufactured in Chicago) and the aid it could provide farmers. He knew that he was out of his home state and didn't have the automatic support of the audience. Even in the birthplace of the Republican Party, there was a sizeable population of Democrats; the rest saw him as a mere also-ran who lost to Douglas. A well-timed speaking tour can do wonders for a presidential candidate, and Lincoln's time outside his own state proved vital, as it increased his name recognition. He spoke to two gatherings of Republicans the following day; his first speech was so strong that he was invited to a neighboring town to give it again.

Lincoln returned to Chicago on October 3. At some point between the summer and November, Joseph Medill stopped supporting Chase of Ohio for president and began to promote Lincoln. It is hard to pin down exactly when his support changed; perhaps it happened face-to-face on one of Lincoln's fall visits that year. At that time, Abraham was not entirely set on running for president (though he knew he would run for some office in 1860), because the office seemed unattainable to him, but Medill's mind was made up.

Abraham was once again in Chicago on November 10 to talk with Judd. While Republican politicians still blamed Judd for the failed Senate race, Abraham stuck by his friend. In correspondence with some of those who still held Judd responsible, Abraham wrote, "The best of us are liable to commit errors, which become apparent, by subsequent development, but I do not know of a single error, even, committed by Mr. Judd, since he and I have acted together politically." In the spirit of this friendship, Abraham gave money to Judd when it was needed. It was just such an occasion when he came to Chicago. Two years earlier, when Lincoln had received his $5,000 check from Illinois Central Railroad, he had invested some of the money in a land venture with Judd, again demonstrating the immense confidence he had in him. His investment was never meant to be permanent, and he now wanted to be bought out. Judd promised him $3,000 with interest and gave a quitclaim deed on land to Lincoln as a security. Judd would still owe this debt when Lincoln was assassinated.

By December, it was certain that Abraham was going to run for the Republican presidential nomination. He himself had thought he would have a better chance at vice president; he thought it impossible to receive the presidential nomination. Medill claims to have talked him out of it. In a conversation with Lincoln, he remembered Lincoln saying, "See here, you *Tribune* boys have got me up a peg too high. How about the vice-presidency— won't that do?" To which Medill responded, "We are not playing second in this dance to any musician. Start in for the vice-presidency, you have lost all chance at a higher place. If you must 'come down a peg,' as you say, it will be mighty easy later on. The Seward fellows would jump at such a chance to get rid of you. But now it is president or nothing. Else you may count the *Tribune* out. We are not fooling away our time and science on the vice-presidency." Medill knew the quality of his man and convinced him to go on another speaking tour outside Illinois to raise his profile before the convention.

The location of the Second Republican Convention was hotly debated. The three front-runners for the nomination were William Seward of New York, Simon Cameron of Pennsylvania and Salmon Chase of Ohio. Each candidate wanted to host the convention in their state, knowing the importance of a friendly crowd. Consequently, they were not willing to place the convention in one of their opponents' strongholds. At the Astor House in New York, on December 21, 1859, members from each Republican state committee met to decide on a location. Judd, as chairman of the Illinois committee, was present, eager for a chance to get it in Chicago. Lincoln was known to those in attendance but was not considered a serious candidate, as he had only served one term in Congress. Cities across the North were suggested, each hoping to have a slight advantage over their opponents. Judd waited until all proposed cities were argued down before offering up Chicago. It was a large city that could hold all the conventiongoers, Judd promised, and its position at the heart of rail lines and waterways meant it would be easy for the candidates to get supporters there. Additionally, Illinois had a large population of Democrats and was a vital swing state to win; perhaps by placing the convention in Chicago, they might galvanize the state's Republicans. In the end, Chicago was picked, winning by just one vote. This was the first national political convention in Chicago, which would go on to host more than any other American city. The representatives of the major candidates thought they had chosen solid neutral ground; none of them realized that Judd had set a trap.

Medill had gone to Washington in early December to talk with congressional leaders about the possibility of a Lincoln nomination. Shortly after his return, he was given a position on the Republican State Central Committee by Judd. Medill was in charge of finances and voters in central Illinois. With his newspaper and power, he began to campaign for Lincoln. As Lincoln's self-appointed manager, Medill had him speaking in neighboring states. Then a golden opportunity landed on his doorstep: Lincoln was invited to speak at Cooper Union, an institute of free learning on Manhattan Island. This was a chance to get recognition in the East and boost his renown.

Abraham spent weeks writing his address. Shortly before heading to New York, Medill would later claim, Lincoln came to the offices of the *Chicago Tribune* to have Medill and his partner Charles Ray look it over. They both agreed that the speech was excellent but offered minor changes to improve the flow. Then Lincoln left for New York. However, Lincoln's journey took him to Indiana from Springfield, and it is likely that he didn't go to the *Tribune* at that time. It is possible that Medill confused the details and edited the speech by correspondence instead of face to face, or perhaps they worked together on some other speech.

Lincoln was the biggest Republican in Illinois and was known in the Northwest, but to the east he had few supporters. His debates with Douglas had been two years earlier, and though he had gained fame for them, he needed to prove he was not just some also-ran. His speech was delivered on the twenty-seventh of February, 1860. In it, Lincoln argued that the Republican Party was a conservative force that was executing the dream of the Founding Fathers and that the South's use of slaves at such a scale was in fact a betrayal of that dream. The speech was picked up by Horace Greeley's *New-York Tribune* and carried all over the North. Greeley, a supporter of Bates of Missouri, praised Lincoln. The Cooper Union Address, as it came to be known, gave Lincoln the recognition he needed in the Northeast. All the North knew the name Lincoln.

One of Lincoln's last visits to Chicago was for the famous Sandbar Case. The U.S. Corps of Army Engineers, while deepening the harbor, had dredged up tons of dirt and added them to the shore, so that Chicago was expanding into the lake. One resident claimed that since the government added to his property, the land was now his, hoping to win six acres of new land. The legal battle had dragged on for years before Lincoln's involvement. The case had a total of nineteen lawyers over the course of the proceedings, including Salmon Chase of Ohio. Lincoln represented the defendants. There exists a full transcript of the case, rare considering fire later burned the records. In it, Lincoln is shown to have a strong sense of deductive reasoning and humor, using both to sway the jury.

When court was not in session, Lincoln kept busy. He was invited to Evanston, where he was entertained at the home of Julius White, an

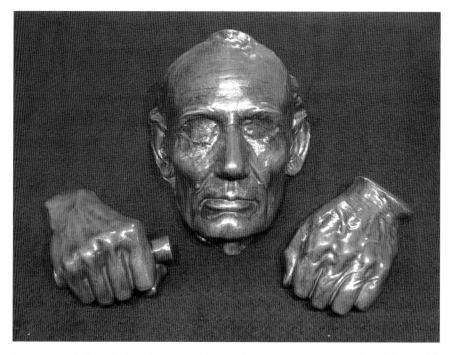

A casting made from the Volk molds. Sculptors and artists have Volk to thank, as it is from his molds than nearly every statue or bust of Abraham Lincoln is made. Volk's wife was Stephen Douglas's cousin, and he did an early mold of the Little Giant. *Glessner House Museum.*

old friend and member of the Chicago Board of Trade, and by college professors from Northwestern University; he also gave sittings for sculptor Leonard Volk. Volk had done a bust of Douglas and managed to convince Abraham to do one, too. The studio was in the Portland Block, a five-story office and apartment building located on the southeast corner of Dearborn and Washington Streets. Lincoln sat for the mold, or life mask, early in the mornings, before court, and he and Volk told humorous stories to each other while waiting for the mold to set. According to Volk, Lincoln much preferred attending these sessions to his other social obligations, declining an invitation to church and trying to avoid going to the nearby town of Evanston. During one session, when modeling the neck and shoulders, Lincoln took off his jacket and shirt and loosened his undershirt, leaving it hanging during the modeling. When the session was over, Abraham dressed himself and went into the street—only to come back moments later after realizing he hadn't put his undershirt back on and its sleeves were dangling around his waist as he walked down the street. He redressed and went on his way, leaving Volk to laugh. Volk kept his office door locked during the sittings in order to give Abraham some privacy, as many people eager to speak with him gathered in the hall. When the bust was finished, Abraham brought Chicago friends, such as Ebenezer Peck, to view the likeness, and everyone agreed it was excellent.

In the end, the court found for Lincoln's client, and he left the city. In a few months, the Republicans would decide their nominee in Chicago, and while the city would have a pull on him for the rest of his life, he would only return there twice more: once as the president-elect and the last time in a coffin.

Chapter 5

CHICAGO'S CHOICE

*L*ate November 1859, about the time when Judd laid his trap hidden in the innocuous suggestion of Chicago, his personal feud with its mayor, John Wentworth, was causing problems for Illinois Republicans. Judd and Wentworth had both started out as Democrats with Free-Soil leanings and a love for the wheeling and dealing of politics. The source of their animosity was personal rather than political, and as the years passed, their dislike for each other only grew. When Douglas passed his Kansas-Nebraska Act, both Judd and Wentworth jumped ship and joined the newly formed Republican Party. Despite this, their enmity for one another persisted as they both became politically powerful and factions arose. Judd had opposed Wentworth's first campaign for mayor alongside a number of Chicago Republicans, Wentworth being an unwelcome member of the party in their eyes. Almost immediately after his election, Judd and other established party leaders wanted Wentworth gone. Judd knew Medill well, and the *Chicago Tribune* was on his side. Wentworth, in the face of such opposition, did not run for reelection. As Judd rose to become the chairman of the state Republican committee, Wentworth went on the attack. He used his paper, the *Chicago Democrat*, to denounce everything that Judd had ever done. Judd was held responsible for the loss of Lincoln's Senate race in 1858; for defeating Lincoln's first campaign for senate in 1854, obstinately holding his votes for Trumbull; for perceived corruption; and for close ties with Governor Joel Matteson, who had defrauded the treasury. Judd returned from New York outraged and sued for libel. Caught between them was their mutual friend and ally, now the most famous Republican in Illinois, Abraham Lincoln.

Lincoln was off in Kansas delivering a speech as part of a profile-raising tour that would cover four thousand miles and deliver twenty-three speeches in one year, unaware of the storm brewing back in Illinois. Wentworth, having just won his second term as mayor of Chicago after a year out of office, was well situated to interrupt the Republican fortunes in the upcoming 1860 election by withholding the city's support; a split would deliver the Democrats Chicago and Illinois. Both factions sent word to Lincoln, each hoping that he would support them and oust the other, and Wentworth asked for Lincoln to represent him in court. Returning, Lincoln played peacemaker. He was certain he was going to run for president and needed both Wentworth and Judd on his side; a failure to win Chicago would be fatal to his campaign. He refused to force Wentworth out and supported him, but at the same time, he wrote a letter to Judd absolving Judd of all blame for his previous electoral failures. His personal appeals to both camps settled the feud, and Judd dropped the lawsuit. It would flare up again only after Lincoln's death.

Republican turmoil calmed, and the people around Lincoln began to plan for victory. Judd had promised party bosses that a grand convention hall would be built that could seat conventiongoers comfortably and that there were plenty of hotels to host them all. He arranged for transport and negotiated for cheaper rail prices. The best deals were for Lincoln supporters, as ticket prices in Illinois and Indiana were especially lowered. John Wentworth promised $5,000 for the construction of the convention hall, to be built in a western style. Medill began churning out praise for Lincoln, and the *Chicago Tribune* followed his speaking tour, printing his speeches in full to ensure Illinois was solidly behind him. In a crowded Republican field, Lincoln needed all the support he could get.

The crowd of potential Republican nominees was full of well-known statesmen, but one stood above the rest. William H. Seward was perhaps the most famous politician the young Republican Party had. A two-term governor of New York and two term senator, Seward had been the strongest voice opposing slavery since 1839. He had passed numerous laws to combat slavery, granting fugitive slaves a trial before they could be taken back. He had denounced the Know-Nothing Party for their anti-immigrant standing. He had powerful, rich backers in New York. On the floor of the Senate, Seward fought Douglas over the Kansas-Nebraska Act. Slavery was to be contained and Free-Soil expanded. All the Republicans knew that Seward was the front-runner; the Northeast was solidly in his pocket, as well as the states of Michigan and Wisconsin.

But Seward's national fame and well-known positions were a concern. He saw a future conflict brewing between the states, calling it "irrepressible," which outraged the South. Rumors swirled about corruption and shady deals. Whichever candidate won the nomination would have to carry every state north of Kentucky. The Republicans were not going to win any southern states with their platform so set against slavery. The key battleground states that had to be won were Illinois (home of the ever-victorious Douglas), Indiana, New Jersey and Pennsylvania. Republicans in these states worried that Seward had already damaged his chances of victory in these states due to his positions. It was his speeches that abolitionists quoted, his words on their banners. He was a liberal spender running in conservative states. He was seen as the hard Radical Republican, though in reality he was more moderate. Even with so many set against him, the pro-Seward delegates would enter the convention with a large bloc of votes.

From Pennsylvania, Simon Cameron must have known that it would be a long shot. He had the backing of the second-largest state in the North, but little else. He was a two-time senator and had changed parties three times, from Democrat to Know-Nothing to Republican. The preferred candidate from an important battleground state, he could expect anti-Seward forces to woo his delegation and perhaps that he'd get a job in the new administration. But his Know-Nothing past made him untouchable to many immigrants.

Salmon Chase from Ohio had higher hopes. He represented the third-largest state in the North and one that could be counted on as solidly Republican. He had been governor of Ohio twice and could reasonably plan on being the anti-Seward candidate, coming in as he did the second-best-known nominee. However, he was coming into the convention with more baggage than he knew. Chase was more radical on slavery than Seward but less well known, ignored by abolitionists. The former Whigs in the party despised him, but he was conservative when it came to spending, and he had not attacked the nativist Know-Nothings. His position may have seemed strong, but his Ohio delegation was not united behind him. Ben Wade and Judge John Mclean (who had penned one of two dissenting opinions on the Dred Scott case) both had their supporters within the delegation. Ohio was not unified, a weakness that could be exploited.

Missouri was hopeful for Edward Bates, a onetime congressman who had only recently joined the party. He was a famous lawyer, having ensured that in Missouri the child of a freed slave could not be enslaved. But in the aftermath of the collapse of the Whigs, Bates too had joined the radical Know-Nothings, and that party's nativism did not go well with the

Republican immigrant base. Bates had come close to securing St. Louis as the convention site, but it had lost to Chicago. Had his city been chosen, he would have had a strong home field advantage. His supporters hoped that since he came from a slave state, the passions of the South would not be inflamed should he win, as opposed to a Seward victory.

Each of these men had a reasonable chance at securing the nomination, but they carried baggage that they were aware of in varying degrees. Two had been in the orbit of the Know-Nothings. Seward was as hated in the South as Douglas had been in the North after the Kansas-Nebraska Act. His election would certainly cause a secession crisis. Seward would arrive with the most votes, so the anti-Seward forces knew they had to unify quickly before Seward's manager, Thurlow Weed, could secure victory. Each anti-Seward candidate angled to position himself second on the first vote to seem like the only viable alternative.

At a meeting in early February with friends, Lincoln finally agreed to put his name in the race. Shortly afterward, on the sixteenth of the month, Medill ran an editorial in the *Tribune* calling for his nomination. Lincoln did not publicly announce his candidacy, deliberately staying quiet, nor did he request endorsements from the newspapers, letting them come out naturally so his candidacy seemed to be the will of Illinois. Lincoln wrote to Judd requesting help, revealing his modest expectations for the convention:

> *I am not in a position where it would hurt much for me to not be nominated on the national ticket; but I am where it would hurt some for me to not get the Illinois delegates.... Your discomfited assailants are most bitter against me; and they will, for revenge upon me, lay to the Bates egg in the South, and to the Seward egg in the North, and go far toward squeezing me out in the middle with nothing. Can you not help me a little in this matter, in your end of the vineyard?*

Illinois had plenty of Republicans, though the northern counties most solidly Republican were for Seward. While Lincoln's strategy of public silence kept his opponents in the dark, it was difficult to maintain the political base he needed at the same time. Judd was the man who could do it.

There was a strong feeling that the Republicans could win with the right man. In April, the Democratic National Convention had met in Charleston. Stephen Douglas entered much like Seward would, with the largest bloc of votes. Worryingly, when the party platform was amended to avoid strong proslavery language for fear of losing the North, the delegations from the Deep South walked out. Douglas was the front-runner on over fifty ballots but was not able to gain a majority, being at best fifty votes short. The southern delegates had not forgiven Douglas for the Freeport Doctrine. Unable to win in the face of such obstinate opposition, Douglas and the National Committee decided to adjourn and try again in a friendlier city. The writing was on the wall; whoever won in Chicago could exploit these divisions.

The Illinois Republican State Convention met in Decatur on the ninth and tenth of May. Here, the delegates would be selected and their nominee chosen. Judd did not let Lincoln down, bringing the convention to nominate him quickly and shocking the strong Seward force from northern Illinois. Any chance that Seward's men could carry the state ended when Lincoln's cousin John Hanks was invited to the platform and unveiled a banner held by two fence posts that read "Abraham Lincoln, the Rail Candidate for President in 1860." The fence posts were some of those that he and Abraham had split in their youth. The crowd went wild, and Lincoln won his state's nomination. From then on, he was referred to as the Rail Splitter; his humble youth was raised up as the paragon of Free-Soil and honest labor. Supporters wrote to Hanks to buy fence posts that Lincoln had split in his youth; each came with a certificate of authenticity.

Twenty-two Illinois delegates would be sent to the convention; among them were Norman Judd, Judge David Davis, Judge Stephan Logan, Leonard Swett, Ward Hill Lamon and Gustave Koerner. But of the delegates from Illinois, eight wanted Seward. If Lincoln did not have a viable chance at winning, they would jump ship. It was vital that he poll well on the first ballot. With the convention one week away, Lincoln's team got to work.

A few weeks earlier, the convention hall was completed. On the corner of Lake and Market Streets (now Lake and Wacker), at the site of the old Sauganash Hotel, stood the massive building that could accommodate ten thousand people, with viewing galleries for the public. The second floor was reserved for men escorting a lady, a ploy aimed at reducing the number of out-of-town men—who would come alone—present. The hall had large windows to allow light and fresh air in, so that even with the massive crowd, it was not uncomfortable. Three sides were wood, while the fourth was brick. Against the brick wall was the speaker's platform, set on wheels, which could be moved around the hall. It had been decorated red, white and blue by a committee headed by Harriet Seward Brown, wife of William Brown and cousin of William Seward. The convention hall was called the Wigwam because all the big chiefs of the party were to gather for a powwow. Wentworth's $5,000 could not buy enough chairs for the event, so Chicagoans lent their own. Chicago, having come so far so quickly in its short history, was eager to show off to all the nation. Excitement reached a fever pitch in the days leading up to the convention, egged on by Medill.

As each day passed, unprecedented numbers of people came into town. Chicagoans watched as trains unloaded thousands of visitors carrying colorful banners, instruments and crates of alcohol. In all, forty thousand people would descend on Chicago for that weekend, a sign of the momentum ready to take the presidency. Hotels charged between $1.50 and $2.50 a night. Accommodations fell short of Judd's promise; there simply was not enough room. At night, people slept on pool tables and in the halls. Nathaniel McLean, son of possible nominee Supreme Court justice John McLean, wrote that "it was almost impossible to move about in the halls without tearing off the buttons from your coat." Reporters from north and

Above: The Wigwam from the street. The hastily constructed building was built to host the 1860 Republican Convention. Here, David Davis and others got Lincoln nominated. The wooden building was retail space until its demolition in 1867. *Alexander Hessler*, McClure's Magazine, *February 1907.*

Following: A drawing of the inside of the Wigwam from *Harper's Weekly* magazine. On the third day, most of the people in the building were Lincoln supporters. The decorations were done by the Republican women of Chicago, led by Harriet Seward Brown. *Library of Congress, Prints and Photographs, LC-USZ62-132553.*

THE REPUBLICANS IN NOMINATING C

IEIR WIGWAM AT CHICAGO, MAY, 1860.

south were all around: the convention hall had a press box for ninety, but six hundred came. The streets were packed as the visitors walked the new city. The majority were the shouters brought by the candidates, people who would scream and cheer at every mention of their man. It was considered poor form for candidates to attend the convention themselves, so instead they sent campaign managers with one goal in mind: secure the nomination by any means.

Among the crowd was Horace Greeley. Greeley had been blocked from going as a delegate of New York by Seward's campaign manager, Thurlow Weed, so he went as a substitute delegate from Oregon. He was strongly opposed to Seward, fearing that he could not carry all the North. He supported Edward Bates as the man who could.

Thurlow Weed, a newspaperman from Albany, New York, was well prepared for the convention. In train car after train car, he brought Seward supporters to Chicago, serving them oysters and champagne the entire journey. Seward was waiting at his country estate, telegraph close at hand so that he could send his acceptance speech immediately. Two thousand dedicated shouters came for Seward, as well as a band in scarlet and white that would play his campaign song "Oh Isn't He a Darling" through the streets of Chicago. Weed had one goal: to nominate Seward as quickly as possible. He knew the opposition that faced him; he knew he needed to win before a divided field could unite. Arriving in town, Weed set up shop at the Richmond House Hotel and prepared for the fight. Seward's shouters were given plenty to drink. Weed had half a million dollars to win the nomination with. Any delegate who met with him was treated to yet more champagne.

Shouters for all the major candidates were in town. Anyone walking the streets in mid-May would have been bombarded by shouts for Seward, Bates, Cameron and Chase, but conspicuously few for Lincoln. Judd and Davis had prepared thousands of shouters, but these men were not deployed in the streets—not yet. Judge Davis, who was chosen to lead the campaign, was saving them for the convention. Demonstrating his knowledge of the political landscape, he had headquarters set up in the Tremont House, a hub of Chicago political life where many of the delegates were staying. They rented the entire third floor as a campaign headquarters, for a total of $300. Davis wrote of the week leading up to the convention, "We are quiet but moving heaven and Earth. Nothing will beat us but old fogy politicians."

The Lincoln campaign left nothing to chance. According to his son, Judd rigged the seating arrangements. He placed the New York delegates loyal to Seward on one side, surrounded by those states that Seward had already won, but placed the swing states next to the Illinois delegation on the other side of the hall. With the second-largest number of delegates, Pennsylvania was sandwiched between Illinois and the sympathetic Indiana seats—which, due to Abraham's time as a Hoosier boy, Davis and Judd felt confident in winning over. Seward's delegates had to cross the entire Wigwam to talk to the uncommitted voters, under the watchful eyes of Lincoln's men.

The only overt moves from the Lincoln group in the days before the convention were made by Medill. On the eve of the convention's start, the *Tribune*'s headline read "The Winning Man—Abraham Lincoln." Medill, though not a delegate, would take his place with the Ohio delegation, many of whom he had known from his time in Cleveland. If Chase's nomination never got off the ground, Medill was well placed to bring the Ohioans over to Lincoln.

The convention opened shortly after noon on Wednesday, May 16. The out-of-town crowd crammed into the hall; those who could not get in listened for news outside. All Chicago desired to see the spectacle—the largest crowd the city had ever seen up to that point. The balloting would take place on the third day; the first two were dedicated to platform and procedure. Even so, on the first day, the Wigwam was packed, ten thousand seats filled and all standing room taken. The Committee of Credentials worked to decide which states and territories could legitimately vote on policy and balloting. Six delegates had arrived from Texas, their status debated, and the territories needed to be assigned seats. In all the hubbub of the opening day, Lincoln's men were quiet; they wanted to run on a moderate platform, but since there were a number of other delegations that needed moderation to carry their states, Davis and Judd could focus their attention on winning the nomination. If Lincoln won, the minutiae of the party's platform would not matter. They had seven cabinet positions to offer, and giving the right one to the right man at the right time could secure victory.

The first two days passed, the platform was decided and the seats given to each delegation settled. Texas and the territories were given permission to vote. After the previous eight years, when the moneyed proslavery interests had won far too often, the Republicans would run hoping to turn back the clock to the Compromise of 1850 and the complete halt to expanding slavery. In addition, they sought high protective tariffs to protect smaller farms and a railroad to California to unite both halves of the nation. The target was the battleground states; the moderate goals were so positioned that opposing them meant supporting the expansion of slavery, and their Free-Soil platform could win the vote of the small farmers.

As soon as the meeting ended on the second day, every delegate's mind turned to the balloting. Indeed, the Seward forces were so eager to nominate their man quickly that they tried to begin voting as soon as the platform was ratified, but this was shot down and the convention adjourned till the next day. The anti-Seward candidates knew that they had to ballot well in the first round in order to stand a chance. To win the nomination, the convention decided a simple majority was sufficient: 233 of 465 votes. The three largest state delegations were New York with 70, Pennsylvania with 54 and Ohio with 46. Lincoln had none of these states, but he did have the best manager at the convention, David Davis.

Davis and Judd met with the Indiana delegation the night before balloting began. They learned that "the whole of Indiana might not be difficult to get." Lincoln was much admired in the state, and his time there as a boy only added to his appeal. Additionally, he was not weighted down by any baggage, he had not disparaged any group in the North and he was preferable to the alternatives. Davis was able to secure Indiana's vote by giving Caleb Smith, head of the delegation, the position of secretary of the interior.

Simultaneously, there was a meeting behind closed doors at the Tremont between the delegations of the swing states in order to decide on a viable candidate who could carry their states. With the Indiana delegation on board, Davis had two of the four states Seward could not win. Still there was no consensus, until it was proposed that Pennsylvania and New Jersey would vote for their own candidates on the first ballot and then switch to Lincoln on subsequent ballots. Davis promised cabinet positions in return for the switch. Pennsylvania and New Jersey agreed. Around midnight, Medill spotted Davis walking down the steps of the Tremont, having just left this meeting. He asked if Pennsylvania had been secured. "Damned if we haven't got them," Davis said. "How did you get them?" Medill asked. Davis replied simply, "By paying their price." At that point, co-owner of the *Tribune* Dr. Charles Ray came down the steps and joined them. Medill asked him the same question, hoping to get more from him than he had the gruff Davis. "Why, we promised to put Simon Cameron in the Cabinet. They wanted assurances that we represented Lincoln, and he would do as we said." "What have you agreed to give Cameron?" "The Treasury Department." Medill was outraged, "Good heavens! Give Cameron the Treasury Department! What will be left?" But Ray calmed him down with the pragmatism that typified the Lincoln men: "Oh, what is the difference? We are after a bigger thing than that; we want the presidency and the Treasury is not a great stake to pay for it."

Despite securing some hundred-odd votes for Lincoln in later ballots, Davis still had to get enough votes to put Lincoln second on the first. The strategy as outlined by Swett was "to give Lincoln 100 votes on the first ballot, with a certain increase afterward, so that in the convention our fortunes might seem to be rising and thus catch the doubtful." By allowing the other states to bring their votes over later, Davis created a clever illusion that Lincoln would gain strength with each subsequent ballot.

It was a stressful time for the Lincoln men. Leonard Swett said, "I did not, the whole week I was there, sleep two hours a night." Their work was made all the harder by Lincoln, who told them, "I authorize no bargains and will be bound by none," and also, "Make no contracts that will bind me." His men were stunned by Lincoln's obstinacy, and Henry Whitney, who had known Lincoln from his days on the circuit, recalled,

> *Everybody was mad, of course. Here were men working night and day to place him on the highest mountain peak of fame, and he pulling back all he knew how. What was to be done? The bluff Jesse W. Dubois said: "Damn Lincoln!" The polished Swett said, in mellifluous accents: "I am very sure if Lincoln was aware of the necessities—" The critical Logan expectorated viciously, and said, "The main difficulty with Lincoln is—" Herndon ventured: "Now, friend, I'll answer that." But Davis cut the Gordian knot by brushing all aside with: "Lincoln ain't here, and don't know what we have to meet, so we will go ahead, as if we hadn't heard from him, and he must ratify it."*

Davis knew how to play politics and could rely on the strategy of selling cabinet positions for the votes he needed. He also had a diverse group of delegates. Illinois was a young state full of people from the east. Swett was from Maine, Logan from Kentucky, Lamon from Virginia; each was sent to the delegation of their home state to promote their man. Also at the convention were two Republican candidates for governor from Indiana and Pennsylvania who warned that Seward could not win their states. Here, Lincoln's speaking tour worked wonders for his men, especially the Cooper Union Address, which gave him recognition in northeastern states unsure of Seward.

Across town, Thurlow Weed was celebrating the inevitable victory he would win for Seward the next day. The thousands of Seward men were still in the streets cheering, and at daybreak they would march in a triumphal procession from the Richmond to the Wigwam. Yet more champagne and other revelries awaited the delegates who would vote for Seward. Weed and all his friends cooped up at the Richmond could not conceive of failure. Yet had Weed talked to those delegates from the battleground states, he may have been less comfortable. Puritans were upset by the drunken Seward shouters, and the large slush fund that Weed had brought with him only seemed to confirm corruption within Seward's circle, as Judge John Mclean noted: "Buying and selling is I have no doubt a large business, and particularly with the New York politicians."

While Weed celebrated, Davis schemed; securing votes from under Weed's nose was not all he had in store that night. Ward Hill Lamon, a large Virginia lawyer and personal friend of Lincoln's, left the Tremont in the dead of night, headed to a Chicago printer. Prearranged, counterfeit tickets were made for the third day of the convention only. Lamon then took these and gave them to Lincoln supporters, most notably the Wide Awake clubs. Suddenly ten thousand Lincoln shouters were in the city, seemingly from nowhere.

As dawn broke on the eighteenth of May, the Seward supporters gathered for their march to the Wigwam. A large procession worked its way through Chicago with celebratory pomp; Seward men could not conceive of defeat. Their man would win on the first few ballots and then on to Washington. Taking their time, since the balloting would not start till ten, the shouters and the band escorted the Seward delegates at a speed more befitting a funeral. When they finally arrived at the Wigwam, they were shocked to find that their seats had been taken and their tickets were useless. As the delegates went in through a side door, Seward supporters were kept out of the hall by the door men. There was shoving at the doors as Lincoln's men helped keep out Seward's. With all the seats taken on the first floor and all standing room taken, the only available room was in the gallery, but entry was for men accompanied by a woman. So those outside rushed to find a companion, grabbing washerwomen and prostitutes off the streets, sometimes paying them for their company. Even so, few got in.

The confusion David Davis created delayed the start of the convention two hours. When things had settled, the opening benediction was said by the Reverend M. Green of Chicago, and the president of the convention asked the audience to remain quiet—a futile plea, as it would turn out. It had been decided that the nomination speeches would be short, only a sentence or two, so as not to drag out the ordeal. William Evarts of New York stood first and nominated Seward; cheering and applause burst out that lasted several minutes. Next, Judd stood to speak: "I desire on behalf of the delegation from Illinois, to put in nomination, as a candidate for President of the United States, Abraham Lincoln, of Illinois." All at once, half the hall stood and cheered; the official minutes of the convention describe it as "immense." The Lincoln shouters were the loudest people in the state, reputed to be able to shout clear across Lake Michigan. Swett later wrote that "the idea of us Hoosier and Suckers being out screamed would have been bad. Five thousand people leaped to their seats, women not wanting, and the wild yell made vesper breathings of all that had preceded. A thousand steam whistles, ten acres of hotel gongs, a tribe of Comanches might have mingled in the scene unnoticed." The color drained out of the faces of the Seward men. The Lincoln boys had clearly outshouted them. When the delegations of New Jersey, Pennsylvania and Ohio had each nominated their favorite sons, Caleb Smith of Indiana seconded Lincoln's nomination, again to a fantastic uproar. The Seward shouters, sensing that they had lost the yelling competition, went wild when Austin Blair of Michigan seconded Seward's nomination. Seward would receive five nominations and Lincoln four, the most memorable being Columbus Delano of Ohio's: "I rise on behalf of a portion of the delegation from Ohio, to put in nomination the man who knows how to split rails and maul democrats—Abraham Lincoln." The balloting had begun.

The Illinois-Indiana block gave Lincoln forty-eight votes. An additional fifty-four votes came to him from East Coast states, such as Maine and Virginia. As expected, Seward was in the lead with 173.5, but Lincoln had 102. Edward Bates of Missouri had 48, Cameron of Pennsylvania had 50.5, and Chase of Ohio won 49. Forty-two votes scattered to other candidates. Seward was fifty votes shy of the 233 needed to win. Each delegate had one vote, but they could split it in half to vote for two candidates. The lack of cohesion within Ohio was fatal to Chase's campaign; Bates had his home state and the support of Horace Greeley, but little else. Davis had cleared the first hurdle; Lincoln was second to Seward. The Pennsylvania delegation, having voted for their favorite in the first ballot, was now willing to pull for Lincoln. The lead Davis had won galvanized the anti-Seward forces: Lincoln was their best bet for victory.

The second ballot began soon after the totals were announced. Seward gained eleven votes, as some delegates joined for his inevitable victory. But the flip of Pennsylvania and other anti-Seward states gave Lincoln a gain of seventy-nine; he was three-and-a-half votes behind Seward. Chase and Bates weakened as Lincoln became the clear choice. Both front-runners were forty votes shy of winning. The final total of the second ballot was Seward 184.5, Lincoln 181, Chase 42.5 and Bates 35. Horace Greeley's fear that an unstoppable Seward would win before opposition could unite proved unfounded. Just as planned, Lincoln gained steam on the second vote.

The third ballot could break either way. The more radical delegates could go to Seward when presented with a moderate like Lincoln, or perhaps the anti-Seward forces could unite no further, and he would receive no new votes. The entire Wigwam was silent as everyone kept track of the votes in their heads. And when the final delegation had reported their vote, the Lincoln crowd was jubilant. Seward had lost four-and-a-half votes, down to 180. Lincoln, meanwhile, had won 231.5 votes, just 2.5 short of victory. Chase and Bates combined had fewer than fifty votes. Medill, who had played only a small part in securing delegates so far in the convention, was sitting with the Ohio delegation; he turned to D.K. Carter and told him, "If you can throw the Ohio delegation for Lincoln, Chase can have anything he wants." "How do you know?" Carter asked. "I know and I wouldn't promise if I didn't," said Medill. Carter rose, and before the total was announced, stammered, "Mr. Chairman! I-I-I a-arise to announce a ch-change of f-f-four votes f-f-from Mr. Ch-Chase to Mr. Lincoln." There was a dead silence for half a moment, then the crowd erupted in cheers, and delegates rushed forward to switch their votes to the winning man to make the nomination unanimous. Only New York, Michigan and Wisconsin still held out for Seward. Like that, Lincoln was nominated with 349 votes.

A call went up to a man on the roof, who fired a cannon to announce the nomination and shouted down to the tens of thousands of Chicagoans eagerly crowded around the building. They carried the cheer: "Lincoln is nominated!" "Hurrah for the Rail Splitter!" The bells of churches and whistles of steam engines and steamboats carried through the city. Celebrations lasted all day. If anyone had a right to celebrate and relax, it was Davis and his men. Thurlow Weed had come with a massive slush fund of half a million dollars and was willing to hand out cabinet seats like candy. Davis won the nomination spending a little less than seven hundred dollars. He was able to secure victory by promising two cabinet seats; Lincoln could fill the rest. Davis did not know about Medill's promise to the Ohio delegation and would likely have been furious. But at least he knew that some deals had been made. Lincoln had expressly forbidden any dealmaking and was now obligated to give three out of seven cabinet seats. Chase, Cameron and Smith were each expecting positions for their part in the nomination.

In Springfield, Lincoln awaited news of the balloting at the offices of the *Journal* with his friend E.L. Baker. If he was nervous about his prospects, he did not show it; telling stories and joking with ease, he seemed to be perfectly relaxed. At roughly midnight, a boy burst into the office clutching a little yellow telegram addressed simply to "Abe," which read, "We did it. Glory to God." He received another from Judd, "Do not come to Chicago." A cry went up in the office and was carried out into the street, where a crowd had gathered. Lincoln excused himself from the proceedings, saying, "There is a lady over yonder on Eighth Street who is deeply interested in this news, I will carry it to her." Mary's claim that one day her husband would become president had nearly come true.

The crowd now moved to Lincoln's home, where they waited for a speech. A brass band had started to play joyful music, and throughout Springfield, guns were fired in salute. Abraham eventually appeared on his front porch and told the crowd that the victory of that day did not belong to him as a person but rather was a victory for a cause that he represented. He told them that he wished his home was large enough to fit them all. The crowd remained outside his home the rest of the night in revelry.

News that a onetime congressman and Springfield lawyer had won the Republican nomination spread like wildfire through the nation. In the South, there was jubilation, for despite all the troubles the Democrats had had with their own convention, any candidate could beat the inexperienced Lincoln. There was a little head-scratching in the North, especially in Seward states. The Lincoln campaign had to bring the big names of the Republican Party into the fold to unite the North. This would prove challenging because while Chase, Bates and Seward had sent letters congratulating Lincoln on his victory, each was bitterly disappointed at his loss. Lincoln set about repairing damaged relationships.

Arriving in Springfield the day of the convention, having heard the news of the nomination while in Bloomington, Leonard Volk went to the Cherney House hotel to dust off and then on to the Lincoln home. Abraham met him on the porch, and Volk said to him, "I am the first man from Chicago, I believe, who has the honor of congratulating you on your nomination for President." They shook hands, and Volk was given a tour of the Lincoln home; a beaming Mary gave him a bouquet of roses. Volk, in turn, presented the family with a cabinet bust of their patriarch, made from Lincoln's life mask.

The day after the convention ended, a delegation from Chicago arrived in Springfield. Led by George Ashmun and Norman Judd, representatives from each state present had arrived to congratulate him and begin planning the campaign. As their train arrived, a large crowd of Springfield Republicans cheered and escorted them to their hotel. From there, the committee went to Lincoln's home, followed by the procession. In the yard, they were greeted by Tad and Willie, who had been waiting to lead them inside. They were introduced to Abraham, who leaned on a chair so as to avoid towering over them. He learned that Hannibal Hamlin of Maine had been chosen as his running mate, to add an eastern name to the ballot. Ashmun formally presented the official nomination, and Lincoln accepted with the remarks that he was "deeply, and even painfully sensible of the great responsibility which is inseparable from that honor…which I could almost wish could have fallen upon some one of the more eminent and experienced statesmen." Lincoln was quite aware that he had not been the first choice for most of his guests, but only a few hours after his nomination, he was already working to reconcile with party leaders. He needed them on his side. After they had met with Lincoln, the group went into the parlor to meet Mrs. Lincoln. Mary was charming when she entertained; she already seemed to be the First Lady. Abraham then shook hands with the several hundred Springfielders as they walked through his home in an orderly line. The following day, Volk made casts of his hands, and his right hand was noticeably swollen from shaking so many hands the day before.

The committee would leave soon after to begin campaigning. Thurlow Weed, at the invitation of Swett, came to Springfield to talk with Lincoln. Weed knew it was important to reconcile the Seward faction with Lincoln. The two of them began to plan. Weed would work on getting Seward to campaign on Lincoln's behalf, which would lock down the Northeast, and Lincoln would find a place in his cabinet for Seward. Lincoln himself would not campaign, would not give speeches or interviews. He would leave that to others, which was common at the time. The nationally circulated platform of the Republican Party would speak for him.

The election of 1860 was perhaps the most consequential in American history. Sectional interests and divisions made it clear to everyone that the next president would have to definitively answer the question of slavery. Having failed to secure a nomination at the Democratic National Convention in Charleston in April, Douglas had the convention reconvene in a friendlier Baltimore, where he was nominated quickly, but worryingly, southern delegations did not attend.

The newly formed Republican Party was for containment. The Democrats, unable to unite, had split, the North behind Douglas and the South for

Vice President John Breckinridge. In the border states, there was the Constitutional Union Party behind John Bell, which wanted to avoid the issue altogether and follow the constitution exactly. It was a divided field, one that the Republicans had no guarantee of winning. While the population of the northern states was twenty-two million and the southern population nine million, half of which were slaves, not everyone in the North would vote Republican. Douglas could win any of the northern states and was Lincoln's biggest concern.

Douglas had his work cut out for him. He had to battle Breckinridge for control of the Democrats and stave off the secessionists, but he also argued that Lincoln's victory would cause a crisis, that he was the only one in the middle. Breaking with tradition, Douglas traveled the country, knowing that he was behind. In the North, he saw Wide Awake clubs marching in the dead of night in torchlit processions for Lincoln; in the South, Breckinridge's speeches were carried in newspapers while his were ignored. Time and time again, he was treated to a lack of interest. Presidential campaigns are built on enthusiasm, and Douglas saw little for himself. Still he soldiered on; he had his supporters across the country and a more impressive record than any of the other candidates. Slowly he came to realize that he would not win. Seeing the writing on the wall, Douglas knew that Lincoln would win the election as early as October, and as the great statesman that he was, he went into the Southern states to convince them to stay in the Union. He argued that Lincoln's victory would not mean the end of slavery and spoke harshly of those who would leave the Union, calling them traitors and promising to hang them. It was a bleak campaign for Douglas; he had too few funds and not much help from the press, but he continued on.

Election Day came on Tuesday, November 6, and saw one of the highest voter turnouts in American history. Voters were eager to defend their sectional way of life against encroachment. Before the voting reform of the 1880s, voters brought their own ballots, printed by the party they would vote for. Sympathetic newspapers printed out the ballots, each color-coded for the illiterate. All voters had to do was pick up a ballot, bring it to the courthouse and place it in the ballot box. The idea was that everyone could see who was voting for whom, and things would be kept honest. That day, Lincoln was at his office in the statehouse surrounded by friends, hiding his nerves with comfortable chat. He had not planned to vote, thinking it dishonest for a candidate to select his own electors, but his partner Herndon managed to convince him to go. The group drew a large crowd as they went to the vote. Lincoln was, after all, one of the first presidential candidates from the West. Roughly around three in the afternoon, Lincoln cut his name off the ballot page (so as not to vote for himself, which he thought dishonest), then dropped his ticket in. Afterwards he went home for dinner with his family, then went to the telegraph office to hear the returns.

Lincoln had lost Sangamon County to Douglas, though he had won Springfield. Throughout southern Illinois, Douglas supporters had voted in droves, and Lincoln had not carried a single county. But north of the Sangamon River, Lincoln won big. Chicago gave Cook County to Lincoln, and he won Illinois by 12,000 votes; 10,697 Chicagoans voted for him. In the battleground states that Seward could have lost, Lincoln was victorious. He had secured all the states north of Kentucky by nine in the evening, with only New York yet to report. Nothing came south of the Ohio River. He had 145 electoral votes and needed 7 more to win. The Republican Party had not found a newspaper in the South willing to print their ballots, so it was New York or defeat, but still no word came, and Lincoln began to fear failure. How many times had he come so close to victory and still lost at the last second? Around eleven thirty at night, the telegraph sprang to life with a message from New York; it read, "The city returns are not sufficiently forward to make us sure of the result, although we are quite sanguine a great victory had been won." He had lost New York City (where city elites thought he would damage the cotton sales, and the poor worried emancipation would mean competing with free Black labor) but won everywhere else in the state. Lincoln was elected the sixteenth president of the United States. Church bells and cannons went mad, and the crowd in the streets began to cheer wildly. Rising from his sofa, Lincoln went home to tell his nervous wife, "Mary, Mary, we are elected." From the noise in the street, she already knew.

Lincoln had won the election, but not by a comfortable margin. Sixty percent of Americans had voted against him, and he had not received a single vote farther south than Virginia, where he received two thousand. He had a total of 180 electoral votes and a plurality of the popular vote. Douglas came second in the popular vote, but it had been so far spread out that he only counted 13 electoral votes. Breckinridge won all the states that would secede and Maryland, but with 72 votes in the Electoral College and eighteen percent of the popular vote, he was far from victory. The Constitutional Union Party won three of the border states with twelve percent of the popular vote. Lincoln worried that his election would be blocked at the last moment by electors or the proslavery senators, but Vice President Breckinridge confirmed the electoral votes, and Southern senators did not object. In an election of sectional interests, the North had undeniably won. Throughout the South, talk of secession intensified.

Now came the difficult task of assembling a cabinet. Lincoln had agreed to honor those deals made by Davis and Medill, seeing the wisdom in keeping the Republican bosses happy. Lincoln was shackled by the conventions of his time. Standard political practice was to hand out cabinet positions and other appointments as favors; no one region or state should be given too many. Those around him, especially Medill (who was hard-set against Seward), wanted Lincoln to appoint their faction to all the best jobs, but Lincoln would not. The president-elect organized a meeting with his running mate in order to get the man he knew he needed, William Seward.

Abraham and Mary went to Chicago on November 21 to meet Mr. Hamlin of Maine and begin planning their administration. Lincoln had also invited Joshua Speed to visit the city with his wife. Upon his arrival in Chicago, Hannibal Hamlin had already decided that he would do whatever Lincoln asked of him. The role the constitution gave to the vice president was quite small: president of the Senate but unable to vote. It was a legislative position; the president did not need to see his vice president during his term. From the train, Hamlin went straight to the Tremont House, where he was to meet Lincoln. The Springfield party came in slightly later. Upon meeting the president-elect, Hamlin was pleasantly surprised; Lincoln wanted his input on his cabinet choices and earnestly listened to his advice. He gave Hamlin the task of finding someone from the Northeast to fit into his cabinet, as well as feeling out Seward for secretary of state.

The next day, the party left the Tremont to tour the city. They visited the Wigwam, site of their nomination, as well as the post office, the customs house and the federal courthouse. Hamlin was impressed by the young city. With their tour over, and after Lincoln got a new suit for his inauguration from tailors Titsworth & Brother, the work of the week began. As Mary went shopping (probably to Chicago institutions such as C.D. Peacock Jewelers and Potter Palmer), Lincoln, Hamlin and Trumbull decided who would get what. The negotiations took much of their time, with the days given to receptions and the afternoons devoted to perfecting the appointments.

On November 23, despite the heavy autumn snow, the people of Chicago went to the Tremont House for a meet and greet, the line stretching out the door and through the streets. Lincoln shook hands with nearly three thousand people for three hours. Mary stood to his right and Hamlin on her right. At one point, after a number of shorter people shook his hand, Lincoln stooping down to their level, a gentleman who was Lincoln's height came in. Abraham's face lit up with a smile, and he exclaimed, "You are up some!"—much to the amusement of the crowd. Abraham did not follow the rules of his own meet and greet; when he saw people he knew, he would pull them out of line and have them stand next to him—and he knew quite a few Chicagoans. After it was over, Lincoln went to dinner with Hamlin and Trumbull, again discussing cabinet appointments. Chicago was full at the time of office seekers, each hanging around the Tremont hoping to get a job in his administration. They pestered him constantly; newspaper reporters joined them to hear the latest rumors.

Amid all the political balancing, reporters and men begging for office, it was a relief for him when Joshua Speed came into town. Lincoln had not seen Speed since his visit to Speed's plantation in 1841, their relationship maintained only through letters. Their lives had diverged some time ago—Speed was, after all, a slave owner—but at the reunion, their friendship was easily rekindled. With Mary and Fanny, Speed's wife, in the sitting room, the old friends went into the bedroom, where Lincoln immediately flopped down on the bed. Lincoln, whose cabinet now looked to contain many political rivals and few friends, asked Speed the innocent question, "Speed what are your pecuniary Conditions—are you rich or poor?" To which Speed replied, "Mr. President, I think I know what you wish. I'll speak Candidly to you—My pecuniary Conditions are good—I do not think you have any office within your gift that I can afford to take." Rebuffed, Lincoln stayed behind as the Speeds and Mary went on a tour of Chicago.

On the twenty-fourth of November, Lincoln surprised people by staying extra days; all the office seekers had gone home, thinking Lincoln would, too. That day he spent totally secluded on North Clark Street and Fullerton Avenue, in the home of Ebenezer Peck, a longtime supporter. Hamlin was with him as once again the cabinet was discussed. Competing Republican factions wanted their men given the top jobs; secretary of state was the largest prize. Medill in particular wanted his close friends around the president and was deeply upset when he learned the cabinet choices, saying, "We made Abe and by G— we can unmake him."

Lincoln's last full day in Chicago was Sunday, November 25, 1860. Along with Hamlin and a friend, Isaac Arnold, he attended a service at St. James Church, today the Episcopal Cathedral of Chicago. Afterward, at the behest of John Farwell, he went to speak to the orphaned children at North Market Mission Sabbath School. There he told the children that if they worked hard and obeyed their teachers, learning all they could, then they, too, might become president. He left to rapturous applause. From there, he went to the photography studio of Samuel Altschuler, who had taken his picture three years earlier. The photo taken shows his half-grown beard and a well-lined face. All his life he had been clean-shaven, but at the recommendation of one Grace Bedell, a young girl in New York, who thought that presidents should have whiskers, he grew his beard.

At a farewell party that night, hosted by William Brown and his wife, Abraham and Mary were treated by the well-to-do of Chicago. It was a grand party on South Michigan Avenue, the city eager for their favorite, Uncle Abe of the West, to set things straight in Washington. There were no speeches, for Abraham rarely gave a speech that he didn't prepare for, just an earnest celebration of their victory. Almost certainly at the party were the wealthy Honoré family, who lived just down the block.

The first picture of Abraham with his beard, taken in Chicago in Samuel Altschuler's studio. He grew it after Grace Bedell sent him a letter, telling him that whiskers would make him look more respectable. *Library of Congress, LC-USZ62-15984.*

As dawn broke the following morning, Abraham and Mary boarded a train for Springfield, and in a few short months, it would be on to Washington, D.C. In his life, he had visited Chicago approximately twenty-three times. He had witnessed as a fur-trapping town got its first railroad and from there exploded into a production powerhouse. Upon his first arrival, there were twenty-five thousand people; when his train pulled away, he was leaving a city of over one hundred thousand. He would never see Chicago again.

Chapter 6

THE WEST IN THE WHITE HOUSE

aiting in Springfield for his March inauguration, Abraham gave no speeches or interviews; he spent his time forming his cabinet. Word reached him that Hannibal Hamlin had been successful on his mission and William Seward was willing to be his secretary of state. For his part, Seward thought he could run things through the inexperienced Lincoln.

While Lincoln was preparing for his administration from Springfield, events began to move quickly throughout the country. On December 20, 1860, South Carolina announced that it would be leaving the Union, afraid that a Lincoln presidency meant the end of slavery. The Buchannan administration adopted a half-hearted position, declaring secession illegal but beginning to consider withdrawing federal garrisons from the South, including Fort Sumter. In all, seven states declared secession before Lincoln took the oath of office.

Secession from the union was an idea nearly as old as the nation itself. The weak Articles of Confederation gave the states a large degree of freedom on all matters but foreign policy. The stronger Constitution did away with this, but the states resented their loss of power, and occasionally talk of secession would flare up in states upset with a law. In 1832, Vice President John C. Calhoun threatened to lead the secession of South Carolina unless Andrew Jackson lowered tariffs.

Lincoln was helpless to stop the seceding states, as he would take office the fourth of March, and the lame-duck president Buchanan was seemingly willing to leave the mess to the next guy. Lincoln worked hard to make his administration moderate and inoffensive to Southerners, taking care not to appoint Northerners to Southern positions. By mid-January, he had finalized his decisions. To advise him, Lincoln had selected each of his Wigwam opponents, obliged by promises he didn't make. William Seward would be secretary of state; Bates of Missouri would be his attorney general. Secretary of the Navy Gideon Welles and Postmaster General Montgomery Blair were both chosen for their Democrat roots and for Blair's popularity in the border states. The three cabinet appointees selected to fulfill promises made in Chicago, Caleb B. Smith, Simon Cameron and Salmon Chase, had been given powerful positions that they were not well suited for. Simon Cameron was given the War Department, something he managed to drive into the ground almost as soon as he arrived. That Lincoln gave such a crucial job to one so unqualified for it indicates that he did not seriously consider conflict between the federal government and the Southern states. Of those three, only Secretary of the Treasury Chase would last more than a year. Surrounded by political rivals, Abraham had no one he could confide in, and a deep depression overcame him soon after he arrived in Washington.

In late January 1860, Lincoln left home for Coles County, Illinois. There, in the log cabin that he helped build with his father, Sarah Bush Lincoln remained, supported by the Hanks cousins. Abraham and his stepmother had remained close despite his few visits, and he sent money when she asked, as he had done with his father. After their reunion, he went to the small cemetery where his father was buried, a simple marker for his grave. Abraham told his cousins to place a headstone on the grave and that he would pay the bill, but he never sent the promised money, and it would not be placed until after his death. He then returned to the cabin and had one final meal with his extended family. He brought with him a black dress that he gave to his stepmother as a gift, which she was later buried in. The next day, he returned to Springfield to prepare for the journey to Washington.

The Lincoln family began packing, selling off all the furniture they did not want to keep and packing the rest into one room. Their home was rented out, and most of their things were bought by the man who rented the house. Their dog, Fido, was given to Springfield friends to look after. Shortly before everything was packed up, the family held a reception for the political class of Illinois. Seven hundred people came, elegantly dressed for the occasion. Mary was assisted by her sisters, and they did not fail to impress. Mary's entire education as a member of the Kentucky gentry was all about how to host social events, and the event at the Lincolns' wowed their guests. More gathered outside the home and cheered for the president-elect. Three days before leaving for the inauguration, the Lincolns left their home and went to stay at the Chenery House hotel.

Abraham was receiving a flurry of mail at this time: insults and death threats that upset Mary deeply but also support and encouragement from across the North. A prominent member of the small but thriving Jewish community of Chicago, a city official by the name of Abraham Kohn, presented him an American flag inscribed with Hebrew from the Book of Joshua. Lincoln took the flag with him to Washington. Many had fought in the Revolutions of 1848 and fled to America after defeat, or else from the wave of persecutions that followed, oftentimes with nothing more than the clothes on their backs and a backpack. They were loyal to the Union for giving them rights they were denied in Europe and supported the Underground Railroad, sympathetic to the plight of slaves. Jewish immigrants had been prominent Lincoln supporters in the election.

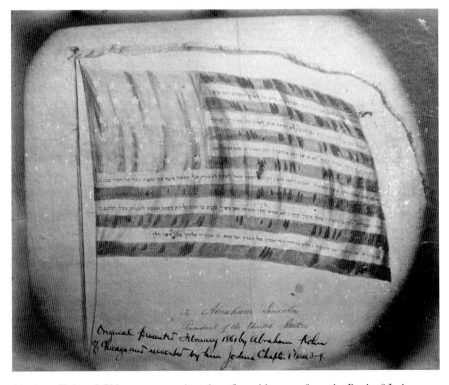

Abraham Kohn of Chicago gave an American flag with verses from the Book of Joshua to Abraham Lincoln on the occasion of his departure for Washington. The verses read, in part: "Be strong and of good courage. Be not afraid, neither be thou dismayed, for the Lord thy God is with thee, whithersoever thou goest." Joshua 1:9. *Newberry Library.*

Abraham began to say his farewells. He told Bill Herndon to keep the law office open; he would pick up where he left off when he came back. His neighbor James Gourley congratulated him, whereupon Lincoln said, "Jim, we have been good friends and neighbors for many years and your family has bestowed many kindnesses on mine. Is there anything I might do for you?" Mr. Gourley replied, "I don't need anything, but it would be nice if you could give my son Harrison a lift." Soon after Lincoln arrived in Washington, he appointed Harrison W. Gourley, who had attended law school and had worked in Lincoln's law practice, as controller and special deputy naval officer in New York City, where he served many years.

On February 11, 1861, the Lincolns left for Washington. In his final address to the people of Springfield, given at the rail platform, Lincoln bid a fond farewell and asked for their support on the challenging road ahead:

> *My friends, no one, not in my situation, can appreciate my feeling of sadness at this parting. To this place and the kindness of these people, I owe everything. Here I have lived a quarter of a century, and have passed from a young to an old man. Here my children have been born, and one is buried. I now leave, not knowing when, or whether ever, I may return, with a task before me greater than that which rested upon Washington. Without the assistance of that Divine Being who ever attended him, I cannot succeed. With that assistance I cannot fail. Trusting in Him who can go with me, and remain with you, and be everywhere for good, let us confidently hope that all will yet be well. To His care commending you, as I hope in your prayers you will commend me, I bid you an affectionate farewell.*

With that, he left Springfield and Illinois, never to see them again. The trip was made in a special train car that he would not leave for much of the trip. Joining him were his family; many notable Northern politicians; his two private secretaries, John Hay and John Nicolay; David Davis; Elmer Ellsworth; Ward Hill Lamon (his self-appointed bodyguard); the detective Allan Pinkerton; and others. The entourage had the run of the train. There was an overflowing bar in the saloon car, but Abraham stayed in his compartment, writing the various speeches he would give along the way. There were many stops, as the train needed to refuel and take on food and supplies. He gave nine speeches in eleven days, touring through the great cities of the North. Springfield, Indianapolis, Cincinnati, Pittsburg, Cleveland, Buffalo, Albany, New York City, Philadelphia, Harrisburg, Baltimore and finally to Washington. Every speech was greeted by enthusiastic applause from the large crowds that met him. Each stop he was beset by office seekers asking for positions. At last he began addressing the secessionist crisis. Lincoln would recognize none of the states as independent, but he was eager to assuage their fears. He declared to the nation he would not interfere with slavery where it existed, but it was not enough.

When the train arrived in Philadelphia, Allan Pinkerton grew concerned. His network of agents had heard rumors that in proslavery Baltimore, an attempt would be made on the president-elect's life. While it is uncertain whether any such plot existed, Pinkerton managed to persuade Lincoln that it was necessary to pass through disguised, against the advice of Davis and Lamon, who thought the plot an invention. Lamon told Pinkerton that he would give Lincoln a pair of pistols to defend himself. After Lincoln's speech at Independence Hall, and after he ran the flag up the flagpole, the Lincoln train went to Harrisburg. Here Pinkerton got Lincoln onto an earlier train that would arrive in Baltimore in the middle of the night. The rest of the entourage would follow the schedule as planned. The detective was so convinced of the plot, he had all telegraph lines to Baltimore cut so that no word of the switch could be spread. Pinkerton, Lincoln (who was disguised as an invalid, a female agent acting as his nurse) and another agent came to Baltimore well after nightfall and found no crowds to greet them, all according to plan. But the train to Washington left from a station across town, and due to noise ordinances, no train could go through the city at night. So the detectives gathered up all the horses they could find to pull the train through the city and to the station. Abraham Lincoln arrived in Washington the morning of February 23, 1861, safe and sound.

Meanwhile, his family was pulling into Baltimore, where a hostile crowd had gathered. Shouting "Trot him out" and "We'll give you hell," the unruly mob peered through the windows of the president-elect's car and began walking up and down the halls of the train, trying to find Abraham. Several broke into his car but were quickly pushed out by John Hay. Word spread that Lincoln was already in Washington, and a cry went up for "Bob" Lincoln. Robert, in his first year at Harvard, went out onto the platform to speak, facing the jeers of the hostile crowd, a revolver in his pocket just in case. The soon-to-be First Family took the abuse for half an hour before going to the Eutaw House for a meal with local dignitaries. From there, they were taken to the very same train station Abraham had snuck out of that morning. The crowd had followed them, and as they boarded the train and waited to get on their way, drunks pressed their faces against the glass and heckled them. At four in the afternoon, the First Family arrived at last in Washington.

The next week, the president-elect and his family stayed at the Willard's Hotel. Lincoln met with delegations from the states—but ominously, none from the South. Much of his time was spent with Seward and President Buchanan. All the while, the secession crisis deepened. No action was taken by the administration to fortify federal garrisons in the South. The army numbered roughly sixteen thousand enlisted men and hadn't fought a major conflict in a decade.

On March 4, shortly after lunch, President Buchanan and President-elect Lincoln left the Executive Mansion for the steps of the new Capitol Building, its dome still unfinished. There, in front of thirty thousand people, Abraham Lincoln took the oath of office and became the sixteenth president of the United States. Stepping forward to give his inaugural address, he paused, looking for somewhere to place his hat. Senator Stephen Douglas, who had only months before campaigned to stand in his place, rushed forward and held the hat in his hands for the entire inaugural address, all the while beaming as his friend spoke: a powerful gesture of unity to a troubled nation. Mary's prediction was now realized. The thin farm boy from Kentucky had won despite so many obstacles. He had lost two Senate races, his party and a son. He had been a resounding failure in Congress and a successful railroad lawyer. As president, it seemed that he would have to solve the secession crisis that had been kicked down the road for so long, rather than pursue his own policy.

In his first speech as president, Lincoln held that he had no right to interfere with slavery in the places it already existed, as he was bound by the Constitution, but that he would not permit secession under any circumstances; an attack upon federal property would be an act of rebellion and met with the full force of the army. Nor would he interfere with the Fugitive Slave Act, because it was in the Constitution. The Constitution charged the president with upholding it in its entirety; he could not pick and choose what to enforce. However, he also said that the Constitution explicitly forbade secession. By doing so, he placed the government on the defensive, so that those who would secede would have to attack first. His speech was received around the nation to predictable results. To Republicans, his speech was reasonable and conciliatory, calling for peace when the North had been so frequently attacked. To Democrats, the speech was inflammatory, threatening and authoritarian. Lincoln ended his speech: "We are not enemies, but friends. We must not be enemies. Though passion may have strained it must not break our bonds of affection. The mystic chords of memory, stretching from every battlefield, and patriot grave to every living heart and hearthstone all over this broad land, will yet swell the chorus of the Union, when again touched, as surely they will be, by the better angels of our nature."

That evening, there was a dinner at the Executive Mansion hosted by the First Family for seventeen guests; Buchannan was present. At eleven o'clock, the presidential party arrived at the inaugural ball, which went late into the night. Douglas danced the quadrille with Mary, like they had in her first years in Springfield. Abraham seemed to observers to be distant; undoubtedly, he was already thinking of a solution for the crisis. Mary was positively radiant, the center of attention. She wore a conservative blue dress and danced until nearly four in the morning, three hours after her husband had retired. There had been fears among the eastern elite that the wife of the "Rail Splitter" would dress and behave like a frontier woman and know nothing of proper etiquette, but these were entirely unfounded, and she charmed senators and congressmen with her perfect grace. While Mary and Robert danced through the night, Abraham went back to the White House; almost immediately after he came in, he was given an urgent notice from the

Lincoln's first inauguration, with the Capitol dome under construction. In his inaugural address, Lincoln adamantly maintained that he would not end slavery or harm Southern states. Seven states seceded before the inauguration; four more left after Lincoln called for seventy-five thousand army volunteers. *Library of Congress, LC-USZC4-4583.*

Portraits of the newly inaugurated Abraham Lincoln and his wife. *Left*: Mary is dressed well but not ostentatiously and looks motherly and reserved. Her time in Washington was unpleasant, and she was often a target for criticism. *Right*: Abraham's beard had almost grown in full for his inauguration. The first president to harness the power of the media, he knew the power of photographs and made sure that his supporters had copies of his image. In this portrait, Abraham looks stern and calm, offering solid leadership. *Collection of John Toman.*

commander of Fort Sumter, desperately asking for more supplies. Thirty-eight days later, Fort Sumter was bombarded, and the Civil War began.

So much has been written about the Civil War and Lincoln's administration of it. It is possible to write endlessly on the topic, analyzing every marching order, mistake and triumph. It was the most violent war in American history, with well over one million total casualties. This book will not follow the ever-changing fortunes of the war, focusing instead on Abraham's relationships and Chicago. However, there are some things that require special mention.

In the North, railways were all the same track gauge. A passenger leaving New York could arrive in Chicago without changing trains. In the South, each local railway company had its own track gauge, and they rarely matched with a connecting line. In order to go from Richmond to Vicksburg, a passenger would have to change trains at least three times to accommodate for different gauges. Union tracks ran deep inland, and no place was disconnected, whereas in the Confederacy, railways were not connected to each other, running from plantation to port. In fact, the Confederate constitution forbade building railways between states for commercial purposes, effectively disabling any unity the Confederate states may have had. Goods coming in on one line had

The four-year-long Civil War was witness to many scenes of bloodshed, such as the Battle of Atlanta, depicted in this Kurz & Allison lithograph. The first industrial war was fought by industrial means; new weapons and ammo led to staggeringly high casualties. It remains, to this day, the bloodiest war ever fought by the United States, though most of the deaths came from disease. *Library of Congress,* LC-DIG-pga-01842.

to be transported by teamsters across town to the other; there was no central hub. When the Confederacy tried building central stations, the teamsters rioted. The Confederacy would prove far too slow in moving its men and materials around.

The beginning of the Civil War was when the railroads and grain of the Midwest came together. The rich, easy-to-farm soil provided a stupendous volume of grain: in a two-year span from 1856 to 1857, 175,000 bushels of grain were shipped from Whiteside County alone. The grain went to livestock as well, which in turn provided more food. New machines were perfectly suited for the terrain: the reaper favored the flat prairie, and the rich soil fell right off the John Deere steel plow without the need to stop and clean it. The grain could not have reached those who needed it without the Illinois-Michigan Canal, allowing shipping into the Great Lakes while the lower Mississippi was in Confederate hands. Massive silos were built on waterways to increase the speed with which grain could be shipped. The great volume was used to feed those in the army and those in the cities and

Ulysses S. Grant in Cairo, Illinois. This photo was taken shortly after his promotion to brigadier general. Grant had rejected the rank of colonel, holding out for a higher military rank. Union generals, such as George McLellan, blocked his appointment, and Grant may not have become a general if it wasn't for his friend and patron Congressman Elihu Washburne. *Library of Congress, Prints and Photographs, LC-DIG-ppmsca-55864.*

was sold overseas. The nearby Chicago futures exchange brought money to develop the agricultural sector. Lead mined in Galena and timber logged throughout the Midwest came through Chicago on its way to where it was needed, by boat or by rail. The cash-crop Confederacy had none of this; food shortages quickly set in.

The last piece of the puzzle was Ulysses S. Grant. Grant had left the army six years after the Mexican-American War. He had been stationed far from his family in California, and his desire to be with them meant his resignation. However, civilian life did not work out for him; he failed at farming and real estate and quickly fell into debt. Grant and Lincoln both travelled extensively through northwestern Illinois in the years before the war and knew the area well. Grant went to work at his father's leather shop in Galena. There, he was invited to drill a volunteer militia group called the Jo Daviess Guards, because he walked around town in his blue army coat. When the Civil War began and Lincoln called for seventy-five thousand volunteers, Governor Yates of Illinois invited the militia to Springfield, and Grant went with them. With the support of Congressman Elihu Washburne, Grant was appointed to the office of the adjutant general to the governor, serving as a mustering officer and assistant quartermaster (for which he received an extra two dollars a day) while waiting for a commission. In this capacity, he mustered in ten regiments of volunteers. Grant travelled around Illinois enlisting men and securing supply lines. He organized the war effort, placing the weight of Illinois resources behind the Union. At Morrison in Whiteside County, an unknown Grant gave a speech from the window of his office in the temporary courthouse at 101 Main Street (a permanent courthouse was not completed until after the Civil War); later, when Grant was the leading Union general, residents recognized him in newspapers and only then realized how much he had done for them. Under his direction, towns across Whiteside County gave their complete support to the war effort, raising funds and resources, including a $20,000 pension for widows and orphans. For his efforts (and with help from Congressman Washburne), Grant was given a commission as a brigadier general, establishing his base at Cairo, Illinois, to control the upper Mississippi. He would play a key role in the Union's first major victories at Fort Henry and Fort Donaldson, securing the inland waterways. Grant went from mustering officer to brigadier general in a span of six months. His qualities of aggressiveness, resilience, independence and determination made him Lincoln's favorite and a key factor to Union victory.

Willie Lincoln was, by all accounts, the favorite of both parents. He was intelligent and kind, a lover of animals and pranks. One time, Willie and Tad hid in the attic and pulled all the strings that summoned the staff at the same time, so that the staff burst into the president's office all together, fearing something had gone wrong. Willie loved to learn and was the only child who resembled Abraham in temperament. Willie and Tad ran the White House. They would charge visitors for the right to see the president and burst into cabinet meetings to climb all over their father; office seekers looking to ingratiate themselves with Lincoln would give the boys pets, so that soon there was a veritable zoo roaming the White House lawns. The boys would hitch their goats to sleds to go for a ride. Willie seemed destined to follow the legacy of his father, but it was not to be. Both young boys fell ill early in 1862. The cause is thought to be typhoid fever from the well that drew water from the Potomac; the disease might have come downriver from troops encamped close by. While Tad recovered, Willie did not; he lay in bed for weeks. Robert, hearing the news, came from Boston and stayed with his family while Willie languished. Abraham and Mary rarely left his side, the president distracted from his work. For a brief time, Willie seemed to be recovering, so they resumed their duties, hosting a reception. Periodically, they would leave and check on their son; with each visit he weakened before their eyes. Only a few days later, on February 20, 1862, Willie died.

Mary took the loss hard. After the death of Eddie, she had become deeply religious. After she watched the slow death of her bright boy, Mary became a Spiritualist, looking for a connection with the dead. She would lock herself in her room and would not leave, only occasionally meeting with mystics for comfort. Abraham joined her once, more from a desire to keep an eye on the people taking advantage of his grieving wife than from general interest. He disliked emotion when it came to faith, preferring instead a rational faith based on the study of the Bible. Mary dressed in black for the next two years, coming out of mourning only as her husband ran for reelection. Abraham did not have the luxury of sitting idle; the war to preserve the Union had waxed into a furious conflict throughout the border states. The casualty lists brought him great pain as he thought of all the good men dying for what he believed was a righteous cause. Occasionally, though, he would lock the door to his office and weep for an hour before returning to his duty. It is said that he once went to the crypt where Willie was buried and had the casket opened, just to get one last look at his son.

Tad had lost his best friend, his partner in crime, the one person who could calm him down. However, his brother's death proved to be sobering for him. He was still a prankster, but he acted out less frequently. Tad was closer than ever before to his father and was the only member of the Lincoln family to be photographed with Abraham. Tad was given a uniform by Secretary of War Edwin Stanton, who had replaced Cameron in early 1862, and together he and his father would tour Union camps, the wild Tad quickly becoming a favorite of the soldiers, a sort of mascot. At home, he walked the hallways of the White House as if he were president. He would burst into cabinet meetings and sit on his father's lap, much to the cabinet's annoyance. Once Tad ate all the strawberries set aside for a state dinner. He stayed by his father's side well into the night, and when the president finished his work, he would pick up the sleeping Tad and carry him off to bed.

The election of 1864 saw Abraham reelected handily, running against General George McClellan. Joseph Medill had broken with the president and tried to get Salmon Chase elected, but Chicago supporters would not have it. Lincoln dropped Hannibal Hamlin as vice president and ran with Andrew Johnson, a War Democrat who was serving as military governor of Tennessee, on the National Union Party ticket. While many criticized how Lincoln ran the war, the soldiers fighting it were overwhelmingly for him. Though there were occasional problems with payment, the Union soldiers loved the president and called him Father Abraham. His popularity with the troops contrasted sharply with his reputation on the home front. Democrats in Northern states called him a tyrant, while many Republicans wanted more drastic action on slavery, including many in his cabinet. The Emancipation Proclamation, perhaps the single most famous part of his administration, brought withering criticism from both sides. When the war began, Lincoln did not approach the question of slavery. For him, the war was one to preserve the Union, but as the conflict dragged on, he became convinced of the need for that question to be answered once and for all. His first announcement of the proclamation stunned his cabinet, even the more radical members who had been calling for a measure of this kind for months. Secretary of State Seward begged the president to wait until after a major Union victory, else the document would be seen as a last attempt by a desperate administration. When it was first announced to the public following the Union victory at Antietam, the Radical Republicans were annoyed that it had taken so long for the administration to declare what they thought the war was really about. Joseph Medill was ecstatic, and the *Chicago Tribune* supported the proclamation wholeheartedly, though they, too, wondered why it had taken so long. The other side went ballistic, as one could expect. Copperhead Democrat presses, opposed to the war, saw it as tyranny and the end to any peace. This story would play out many times through Lincoln's first four years, though on a smaller scale. The president was exhausted by the pressure but continued on in the hope for a full, reconciliatory peace. In his second inaugural address, Lincoln called for reconciliation and moderation while calling the Civil War divine retribution for slavery. His faith takes up much of the speech:

> *Both read the same Bible, and pray to the same God; and each invokes His aid against the other. It may seem strange that any men should dare to ask a just God's assistance in wringing their bread from the sweat of other men's faces; but let us judge not that we be not judged....If we shall suppose*

that American Slavery is one of those offences which, in the providence of God, must needs come, but which, having continued through His appointed time, He now wills to remove, and that He gives to both North and South, this terrible war, as the woe due to those by whom the offence came, shall we discern therein any departure from those divine attributes which the believers in a Living God always ascribe to Him?…Yet, if God wills that it continue, until all the wealth piled by the bond-man's two hundred and fifty years of unrequited toil shall be sunk, and until every drop of blood drawn with the lash, shall be paid by another drawn with the sword, as was said three thousand years ago, so still it must be said "the judgments of the Lord, are true and righteous altogether."

From his childhood reading of the Bible and his discussions with Dr. James Smith of Springfield, Abraham came to believe in an engaged God, which is what he means by a "Living God." He believed that God was present in every life, watching over his children and over the nation as a whole. Indeed, Lincoln's God was political in nature and instrumental to the fate of nations, protecting or destroying them as He saw fit. In 1865, Abraham felt that God was at last bringing the conflict to an end. Many times during his first term, he prayed after horrible battles and his generals' incompetence, and finally he stood months away from peace.

The war was, at that point, unwinnable for the Confederacy, but it still had blood left to spill. Grant was engaged in the violent and slow Petersburg campaign, having risen through the ranks in his brilliant campaigning in the western theater to be the commanding general of the U.S. Army. Robert's position on Grant's staff was not cushy; he was expected to work as any other officer. He ran messages across battlefields, witnessing all the horrors of war. Perhaps his most important role was convincing his exhausted father to meet with Grant and observe the final days of the war.

The First Family arrived aboard the *River Queen* in late March, after some confusion regarding travel arrangements. Originally the light fast gunboat *Bat* was to take the president in Spartan style to City Point, which had been much to his liking, but at the last minute, Mary had decided that she would be joining him. The *Bat* was deemed unsuitable for the First Lady, and so the steamboat *River Queen* was brought in. Tad joined them, too, and spent his time aboard the boat investigating every nook and cranny. When they arrived in Virginia, they were greeted by Captain Robert Lincoln in his new uniform. At City Point, Abraham was a hero. General Grant and his wife, Julia, met with the First Family aboard the *River Queen*; Lincoln

The second inauguration of Abraham Lincoln (*center, at podium*). The war was almost over, and Lincoln called for peace and reconciliation. Amazingly, this photo shows six conspirators of the assassination. Wearing a top hat near the statue behind the president is the assassin John Wilkes Booth, while just below the president, facing the crowd, are Lewis Paine (who nearly killed Secretary of State Seward), George Atzerodt, David Herold, John Surratt and Edward Spangler. *Library of Congress, LC-USZ62-1676.*

greeted them personally at the gangplank. He would spend eighteen days shadowing Grant's army, witnessing firsthand the war he had been made to fight. During his time there, he would do little of his work, and his poor health seemed to improve considerably.

Apart from the stress of four years of bloodshed and incompetent generals, the presidency had placed a terrible strain on Lincoln's personal relationships. David Davis found that he did not have much access to the president nor influence on policy, frustrating for the man who thought himself a power behind the throne. Lincoln appointed him to the Supreme Court, but the judge still found it difficult to be heard in the administration. After the Wigwam, where Davis sold cabinet seats against Lincoln's express orders, Lincoln found it hard to trust him. Norman Judd was not included in Lincoln's cabinet because power brokers disliked him, and while he was a loyal political ally, history had shown that he had his own interests. Judd was appointed minister to Prussia, essentially ostracized from the presidency he had orchestrated. Joseph Medill and his *Tribune* defended Lincoln from Democrats while at the same time attacking him for his failure to pursue the Radical Republican platform. As general after general was relieved of command of the Army of the Potomac, Medill called for Lincoln to appoint Grant in their place, but it was only in 1864 that Lincoln did. Indeed, one of the few relationships that was not soured during Lincoln's presidency was his friendship with Joshua Speed, who was vital to keeping Kentucky in the Union. With his ear to the ground, Speed told Lincoln whenever Union officials were upsetting Kentuckians and found loyal locals to fill positions. During the course of the war, Kentucky was a powder keg, but thanks to Speed's practical advice to the president, it never seceded. Washington, D.C., had drained Lincoln of his health, and it was a relief for him to be elsewhere.

The last great battle of the war raged eight miles from City Point. The Siege of Petersburg had dragged on for nine months and was one of the war's bloodiest battles. Grant would ride the many miles of siege lines to plan with his generals; with him went the president. Abraham had been in war in his youth, but the scale of what he witnessed around Richmond was incomparable. More men would die in a single minute than in all of the Black Hawk War. He saw the bloody dead and dying, the bedraggled prisoners captured by the Union, their sallow faces full of worry. General Lee had hoped that his tenacious defense would push Grant away, as it had done with so many other Union armies, but Grant would not let up and pushed forward regardless. Lincoln's growing concern was that Lee would soon abandon the Confederate capital to join an army in North Carolina and drag out final victory.

On the twenty-fifth of March, General Sherman arrived to meet with Grant and plan a trap for Lee. Lincoln invited both generals, along with Rear Admiral David Porter, aboard the *River Queen*. They listened as the president outlined his peace plan. There was to be a general amnesty. Lincoln wanted to repair the damage done as swiftly as possible. As soon as a rebel laid down his arms, he was an American once more. His plan was to rebuild and reunify the nation, not to punish the Confederacy. He knew that punitive measures would only lead to more violence down the line. Of the high-ranking Confederate officials, he knew that there would have to be judgement if they were captured, but he did not want to punish them. He told his generals that it would be best if the Confederate cabinet escaped to Europe without his knowledge, to live there peacefully.

The president's time in Virginia was good for his health but was made harder with the First Lady by his side. Normally, when in public, Mary was charming, the perfect host and her husband's fiercest defender. However, when the president's entourage went to inspect the troops, the ladies, riding in an ambulance, fell behind, and Lincoln started the parade without them. The troops on parade were under the command of General Edward Ord, whose wife, Mary, had cautiously joined the review when it became clear that the First Lady and Julia Grant would not arrive on time, and then only with Abraham's permission. Upon arriving and seeing the pretty Mrs. Ord riding next to the president, Mary poured an unending tirade of abuse on her, shocking those present and leaving Mrs. Ord in tears. Julia Grant attempted to calm her and protect her friend but was unsuccessful. Those around were left "shocked and horrified," as Mary's outburst only ended when she was exhausted. When the party returned to the *River Queen*, Mary gained a second wind and began berating her husband for humiliating her. For the next few days, she would not leave her room. On April 1, Mary went back to Washington, escorted by Secretary of War Stanton. The outburst may have been the result of a migraine brought on by the bumpy ride to the parade grounds, or else one of the mood swings Mary was prone to. Perhaps it was a simple case of jealousy; she may have been frustrated at missing the start of the review and upset to see someone in her place. Whatever the reason, it would have drastic consequences.

Away in Virginia, Lincoln did not have to deal with the mounting stack of paperwork or the never-ending stream of office seekers. His health had improved with his long stay, but while he felt better than he had in a long time, he could not relax. From his new flagship the *Malvern*, Lincoln could hear the final battle of the war raging. Grant finally broke through the Confederate lines in Petersburg; Richmond was now in his grasp. General Lee and the entire Confederate government abandoned the city the next day, setting it ablaze. Union forces put the fires out only once the city surrendered to them. As Grant rushed to cut off Lee's escape in the brilliant Appomattox Campaign, Lincoln went with his son Tad to the captured capital. Rowed to shore amid endless flotsam, mines and unexploded ordnance, the president received a rapturous welcome. Most white inhabitants had left Richmond with Lee's army, so he was greeted by free and enslaved Black laborers. Shouts of "Father Abraham" were much to his liking, while cries of "The Messiah!" were not. It was a short distance to the new Union headquarters, formerly the Confederate White House. Even so, it took them a long time to reach there as the crowd grew larger and larger. Though the city had been captured only the day before, Lincoln was guarded by only a handful of sailors. Admiral Porter said later that "I should have preferred to see the President of the United States entering the subjugated stronghold of the rebels with an escort more befitting his high station, yet that would have looked as if he came as a conqueror.…[He] came instead as a peacemaker, his hand extended to all who desired to take it." Those with him thought they saw gun barrels pointed from windows and shady characters in alleys. They were still in hostile territory. Arriving at the headquarters, Abraham and Tad toured the mansion together. They went into the office of Jefferson Davis, and Lincoln sat down behind the Confederate president's desk, where he asked for a single glass of water. The Black porter brought it along with a bottle of whiskey, courtesy of Mrs. Davis.

The war was finally ending. On April 6, Mary returned to City Point with a group of senators who desired to see Richmond. In Washington and across the North, crowds were ecstatic with each piece of news that heralded the end of the war. Though Lincoln desired to be at City Point to hear from Grant, word that his friend Secretary of State Seward was badly injured in a carriage accident necessitated his return to Washington. He saw Seward on April 9 and spoke of his time in Virginia, trying to distract Seward from his pain. Shortly after he returned to the White House, word came that Lee had surrendered earlier that day to Grant.

Guns went off in Washington as work ground to a halt and celebrations poured out onto the streets. Speeches were given and toasts shared; in the last week of his life, Lincoln gave a number of impromptu speeches from the White House balcony. In each, he called for reconciliation and forgiveness. The war would soon be over, the rebels now their countrymen. Lincoln would return property (excluding slaves) and restore voting rights. He called for the enfranchisement of Black men. In one such speech, John Wilkes Booth was in the crowd. Outraged at the thought of Black voting rights, Booth told his friend that this would be the last speech Lincoln ever made.

The Civil War had changed America, Chicago more than any other city. When war came, Chicago gave much for the Union. Stephen Douglas returned from Washington after the attack on Fort Sumter to prepare his state for war. He had met with Lincoln after his inauguration and outlined strategic locations that the Union could attack to defeat the rebels. He also advised Lincoln to raise an army of volunteers, as the regular army was only sixteen thousand men strong. When Lincoln called for seventy-five thousand volunteers, Douglas advised him to raise two hundred thousand. Arriving home, Douglas gave vast tracts of his land south of Chicago to the army for the training of volunteers. He undoubtedly hoped to see the Union win the conflict, but Douglas would die suddenly in the Tremont House on June 3, 1861. In his memory, the land he gave was named Camp Douglas.

Though initially planned as a training camp, within a year it was converted to a prisoner of war camp and would hold ten thousand men throughout the war. It was poorly managed and unprepared for the volume; nearly half of all its prisoners would die. Union soldiers paroled after surrendering and waiting to be properly exchanged were held there, too, and though they were better cared for, many still died. The citizens of Chicago helped feed and care for those interred there; the Honoré daughters helped raise funds. During the election of 1864, a prison break was organized by Confederate sympathizers in Chicago, but the plan was exposed before they could act. City officials placed Long John Wentworth in charge of the police, and he zealously pursued any trace of Confederates in the city.

Approximately fourteen thousand men from Chicago would serve in the war, including men from a show unit called the U.S. Zouave Cadets of Chicago, led by Elmer Ellsworth. He had studied law under Lincoln's tutelage in Springfield and joined him on his train to Washington. Ellsworth was the first officer killed in the war; he died tearing down a Confederate flag in Alexandria. The small Chicago Jewish community armed a company of ninety-six men, raising $11,000 to outfit them, with a little left over to pay bounties to the unit. This company, called the Concordia Guard, served in the biggest battles of the war, including Chancellorsville, Gettysburg, Chattanooga and Sherman's March to the Sea. Some of the first Chicagoans to volunteer for the army were Jewish. Throughout the North, Jewish communities gave tens of thousands of dollars to the Union, playing an important role in financing the war effort. Around fourteen thousand Chicagoans fought in the war, four thousand of whom died, but Chicago's greatest contribution to the war was in supply.

The nation's great distribution centers were suddenly on the front lines of conflict. The major grain depot of St. Louis could ship up and down the Mississippi, but at the outbreak of war, half the river was suddenly hostile and the route to the sea closed. Missouri itself became a battlefield. Chicago took over this duty and supplied the army with food, shipping fifty-six million bushels of grain during the war. The rich soil and endless raw materials of the Midwest came to Chicago by water or by rail, and the city grew rapidly to handle the volume. Chicagoland businesses got rich requisitioning goods for the army, and the heavy industry manufactured things like rails to help the war effort. Potter Palmer, seeing a conflict coming, bought several warehouses of cotton from New York, and when cotton prices went up with the South seceding, he sold it back for a fortune. McCormick's reaper was praised by Secretary of War Stanton for freeing up thousands of farm hands from labor in the fields to serve in uniform. The five hundred factories of Chicago were quickly converted to make war materials. Livestock from surrounding states were shipped to Chicago to be sent to the army. Hundreds of thousands of animals were slaughtered in Chicago. A second wave of millionaires arose, with names like Phillip Armour. At the end of the war, the massive Union Stock Yards were opened to handle the incredible volume of livestock that moved through the city.

There was no city or state in the North that was made entirely of Republicans or Democrats, and the war and Lincoln's administration of it were constantly debated in the papers. Lincoln's opponent in the 1864 election, General George McClellan, was nominated in Chicago at the Wigwam, just as he had been. As with all the nation, Chicago was divided; a number of riots hit the city during the war. When the Copperhead *Chicago Times* was closed at bayonet point for its outspoken criticism, city Democrats formed a mob and threatened to destroy the Republican *Chicago Tribune* unless the *Times* was reopened. Lincoln allowed the *Times* to continue printing when he learned of the closure.

The war was almost over; Lee had surrendered; it was time for celebration. It was well known that Lincoln would be attending Ford's Theater to see a production of *Our American Cousin* on Good Friday, April 14; his schedule was printed in the papers. Booth decided that this was his chance to strike. He had performed at Ford's Theater many times, occasionally with Lincoln in the audience. He planned to assassinate the entire cabinet and General Grant with his small group of conspirators.

It was a long shot, to be sure. Though the Secret Service was not yet tasked with guarding high-ranking officials, each target would certainly have a couple officers with him. Lincoln had Ward Hill Lamon, the massive Virginian who had been appointed marshal of Washington after Lincoln's inauguration and saw himself as Lincoln's bodyguard. When the president travelled, his usual arrangements called for a cavalry guard. There had been incidents throughout his presidency that could have been attempts on his life, such as when the presidential carriage crashed and Mary was thrown to the pavement or when a sniper shot through Lincoln's hat as he rode unescorted through Washington. His cabinet took his safety seriously, considering the hatred throughout the South. They frequently complained to him about his lax security, but he did not change his ways.

Booth's hatred of Lincoln stemmed from his Southern sympathies. He was raised in the slave state Maryland in a family of thespians, growing up in the shadow of his famous father, Junius Brutus Booth, and brother Edwin. Where his brother was renowned as the premier actor of Shakespearian tragedy, John only captured audiences when in a fit of passion. When performing at Ford's Theater, he would aim all his passion and insults at the president's box where Lincoln and his guests watched, bemused. His hatred of abolitionists was driven to rage when Lincoln suspended the writ of habeas corpus in Maryland; he saw the president as a tyrant who must be stopped to preserve Southern freedom. He and several conspirators began plotting to kidnap Lincoln and deliver him to the Confederacy, but when he heard Lincoln's speech calling for Black enfranchisement, he resolved instead to kill him.

Booth arrived at Ford's Theater in the morning to collect his mail and learned that the president would be in attendance that evening. Those who saw Booth that day remembered how he looked sickly and pale. He left the theater and began setting his plan in motion. Nobody is certain exactly when he returned, but at some point in the afternoon, he bored a hole into the president's box, through which he would be able to see the occupants. He rented a horse and told fellow conspirators to assassinate their targets that night.

Any other night, Booth's chances of success would have been slim. Had Lincoln's overzealous, well-armed bodyguard Ward Hill Lamon been there, he would most likely have stopped Booth the second he entered the box. But Lamon was in Richmond on the president's orders. Lamon told the president not to go to anywhere public while he was gone, but Lincoln didn't listen. Throughout the day, Abraham had asked twelve people to join him and his wife at the theater that night, but they all turned down the offer, commonly citing a well-needed rest as the war drew to a close. Abraham had invited his son Robert, but he had declined in favor of a night drinking with John Hay. There was, however, another reason for not attending. Most of the wives of cabinet members could not stand a single social event with Mary Lincoln. General Grant gave the excuse that he and his wife wanted to see their children in New Jersey and simply could not wait to go, but Julia remembered City Point and Mary's constant yelling and would not go anywhere with her. Secretary of War Stanton also declined; his wife avoided Mary like the plague, though Stanton said he would not go in protest of the president's disregard for his own safety. Had the Grants accompanied them that night, Federal troops would have flooded Ford's Theater as the general's security detail. Stanton, so concerned with security, would have organized a guard.

Instead, the president and his wife went to the theater with Major Henry Rathbone and his fiancée, Clara Harris. One special policeman was assigned to guard the box. The party arrived late and took their seats; the orchestra played "Hail to the Chief" as they entered. Major Rathbone sat with his fiancée on the sofa provided them, the seat furthest from the door. Had he taken up a spot behind Lincoln, he may have been able to stop Booth. At nine thirty, Booth entered the theater through the back but was told he couldn't cross the stage during a scene. He went around to the front and paced around the lobby nervously until ten. He then went to the saloon for a brandy to quiet his nerves. When he finished, he went up to the dress circle and, finding no guards, entered the hallway that led to the box. The officer on duty had left as soon as the president and his guests were seated. It is uncertain where he went that night, but had he done his duty, he might have noticed the sickly Booth and stopped him.

Booth pushed open the door that led to the box and barred it shut behind him with an iron rod. Looking through the peephole he had made earlier that day, he had an unobstructed view of the president: no guards, no one to block his path. He knew the play well, entering the box during the biggest laugh. The last thing Abraham Lincoln heard was the simple American cousin berating a scheming English woman: "Well, I guess I know enough to turn you inside out, old gal; you sockdologizing old man-trap!" Laughing, his head vanished in a puff of smoke as Booth shot from close range. He slumped over immediately as the confused crowd looked to the box.

Rathbone wrestled with Booth before the assassin pulled out a knife and wounded him in the arm. Booth then leapt to the stage but tripped on the banister, landing awkwardly, and broke his leg. He shouted the state motto of Virginia, "Sic Semper Tyrannis": thus ever to tyrants. In a mad dash, he cut his way to the back door and vanished into the night.

Several doctors were in the crowd that night, mostly young army doctors hoping to catch a glimpse of the president. The first was lifted twelve feet in the air so he could reach the box. Wounded, Rathbone unblocked the door to let others in. The doctors knew immediately that Abraham would not survive; the bullet had entered near the left ear and was lodged behind the right eye. He was still alive, but his breathing was weak and shallow. When it became apparent that he would not die immediately, it was decided to move him to a bed. Under the direction of Dr. Leale, who held his head, the procession left the theater and went into the dark street. Henry Safford, a boarder at the Petersen House across the street, cried out, "Bring him here."

A crowd gathered as they brought him into the dark house and laid him down on a bed too small for him. Mary sobbed uncontrollably at her husband's side. As word spread through the city, cabinet members began to arrive, as did Robert and John Hay. Soon, word came that Seward had been attacked as well. The cabinet was in a state of shock, fearing some great conspiracy—all except for Secretary Stanton, who did not have the luxury of worry. He immediately gave orders to block all roads from Washington, organizing a manhunt from the parlor of the Petersen House. It was Stanton who informed Andrew Johnson that he would soon be president. Mary clung to her husband's chest until Stanton had her removed from the room so that the doctors could continue their work. Robert tried to comfort her but was himself inconsolable. The night wore on without a change to the president's condition. Johnson was brought and stood at the bedside, conferring with the cabinet until Mary desired to return to the room. The cabinet knew that she detested Johnson and so had him leave, much to his annoyance.

Around seven in the morning, it became clear that the end was near; his heart grew faint and his breath shallow. Mary was allowed to return as all eyes now watched his struggling chest. At 7:22 in the morning of April 15, 1865, Abraham Lincoln died. Stanton, at the pronouncement, said, "Now he belongs to the ages."

Robert and Mary left the Petersen House for the White House, where they found a distraught Tad. The youngest Lincoln had been at a production of *Aladdin and the Wonderful Lamp* when the manager came on stage and announced to the audience that the president had been shot. Tad immediately stood up and ran screaming through the aisles, "They killed papa! They killed papa!" Mary had wanted to bring Tad to the Petersen House, but those present disagreed. The Lincoln family was down to three, unprepared for life without their patriarch. Robert had not completed law school, putting his education on hold while he served in the army. Tad could not read due to his father's lenient approach to raising children. Mary had become increasingly unstable from the seemingly unrelenting loss of loved ones.

All the nation began to mourn. Though he had his detractors north and south, when the word came of his death, he was eulogized throughout the nation. He was remembered as a compassionate man and the preserver of the Union. Many in the South were outraged by the dishonorable assassination, recognizing that they had lost a great ally in the late president. Lincoln had wanted not to punish the rebels but return them to the nation with their fears assuaged. High-ranking Confederate generals such as Robert E. Lee and Joseph Johnston denounced Booth and expressed their shock. This is not to say that no one celebrated the news; there were those who thought Lincoln was a tyrant and publicly celebrated, but they were by far the minority.

Mary spent days in her room in shock, comforted by her dressmaker. But though she was incapable of anything public, she had to deal with the pressing issue of where her husband would be buried. Many in Congress wanted him to be placed beneath the Capitol rotunda in the space originally intended for George Washington. Mary rejected this out of hand. She hated Washington, D.C., and held the capital responsible for all that had befallen her family. A delegation from Illinois requested that he be buried in their state, to place him at rest where he first rose to prominence. Mary agreed, and she thought Chicago was the likely spot. She had loved the city when they visited, as had her husband. It had played an important backdrop to his rise and influenced him directly. They had even considered moving to Chicago when he was no longer president. In the end, she chose Springfield, though she did not love the town, for it had been their home for twenty years.

Her decision made, work on the tomb went on round the clock, while preparations began for the largest funeral in history. He was embalmed, and for six days after he died, Lincoln was mourned in Washington. There were two public viewings, one in the East Room of the White House, the other in the Capitol Building, attended by tens of thousands. Soldiers came to mourn their fallen chief; he had inspired intense loyalty among the troops. General Grant was inconsolable; tears rolled down his face as he sat in the East Room. Black stood beside white in mourning, and anyone who protested had Secretary Stanton to deal with; he would not refuse anyone who wanted to look at the Great Emancipator. Mary did not come to say goodbye to her husband; it was too much for her. Instead, she was in her room weeping. Her confidant Elizabeth Keckley stayed with her, doing her best to provide comfort. After those six days, the funeral train, draped in black, left Washington on its 1,700-mile journey.

With the final destination Springfield, it was decided that the train would follow his inaugural route in reverse, though Cincinnati was excluded for being too far out of the way and Chicago added due to his relationship with its people. Baltimore, Harrisburg, Philadelphia, New York, Albany, Buffalo, Cleveland, Chicago and finally home to Springfield. Rain seemed to follow the procession, and several of the funerals had smaller turnouts

The Lincoln funeral arrives in Chicago from Indiana. The funeral train is in the background of the photograph, resting on a trestle above Lake Michigan (near where Buckingham Fountain is today); a temporary platform was built over the lake to reach it. The coffin was placed on a dais beneath the great funeral arch. *Library of Congress, LC-DIG-ppmsca-19202.*

than expected. In places along the route where the train would not stop, people lined the railroad to pay their respects. When night fell, the people along the tracks made campfires and lit torches, dotting the fields like stars as they tried to catch a glimpse of Lincoln's train.

In all, seven million people viewed the body, the procession or the train go by. Teddy Roosevelt watched the New York funeral from his grandfather's apartment. James Buchanan, who had left so much of the secession crisis to Lincoln, watched the train pass in Pennsylvania. After the stop in New York, it was decided that they would not show his face, as the decomposition was so advanced. The lid was sealed shut, but the mourning crowds would not have it, demanding to see his face. So, instead, a mortician made sure that Lincoln was presentable before the public was permitted to see him. As the

LINCOLN LYING IN STATE

Above: Crowds of mourning Chicagoans go into the courthouse to view Lincoln's remains. Both the exterior and interior were draped in black. In this courthouse, Abraham argued his most famous cases. A chorus of veterans from the Germania club, three hundred in total, sang at the Chicago courthouse funeral. *Library of Congress, Prints and Photographs, LC-USZC4-1835.*

Left: An embossed Lincoln memento given to Chicagoans, likely during the Lincoln funeral, as the black bars indicate death. The funeral arrived in the morning, and it wasn't until the afternoon that the public was allowed to pay their respects. They were allowed in through the night, and when the funeral left for Springfield, over one hundred thousand had viewed the remains. *Collection of John Toman.*

train wound its way home, his skin turned black, and his body shriveled. With white chalk, they tried to hide the decay; even so, it was noticeable to the mourners. By the end of the journey, his six-foot-four frame, which had only just fit inside the coffin at the beginning, had room to spare.

Where Washington was the grandest, and New York the largest, Chicago was the most heartfelt. The city had given much to the Union cause during the war: land, money and blood all sacrificed at the altar of the nation. As the train arrived in Chicago, it waited on a trestle above Lake Michigan. A platform was built over the lake, and the coffin was taken off the train. The pallbearers were all his close friends, Wentworth among them. Beneath a magnificent Gothic triple arch just off the beach in what was called Dearborn Park (near where Buckingham Fountain is today), the city began to say its farewell. He was eulogized by Chicago politicians just as he had given eulogies for Zachary Taylor and Henry Clay. Thirty-six maidens in white walked beside the coffin, each placing a single flower upon it. Everything was draped in finery, so that the city was colored black, red, white and blue. Slowly, he was moved in a procession down Michigan Avenue, then down Lake Street, avoiding run-down or industrial areas, until the procession came to the courthouse in which he had argued so frequently and successfully. There, the casket was opened, and the people of Chicago filed past, eager for one last glimpse of their hero. It was two weeks since he had been shot, and his body was in a state of distressing decay; many wept at the sight of his shriveled frame. For two days, the solemn line shuffled past him, even through the night. Over one hundred thousand people paid their respects, many had known him in life. At last, it was time to go home: a peaceful last ride from Chicago to Springfield on the train line he had lobbied for himself. Lincoln left Chicago for the last time, but the people of Chicago did not permit him to take this tragic journey without their final gift.

George Pullman, having made a fortune in Chicago raising buildings to accommodate new sewers, had since entered into train manufacturing. He built the most luxurious train cars: the first sleeper cars with washing and dining facilities, with shocks to ease the ride, perfect for the Golden Age of Rail. The Pullman sleeper car was wider than most others, and the platforms had to be moved in advance to accommodate it. Lincoln was placed in one such car, built in Chicago, for the journey from Washington to Springfield. The car had only just been delivered to the president, meant to allow him and his cabinet to travel the country comfortably and safely. It was never used in Lincoln's life. Its first use was taking the slain president on the long journey home.

The funeral train arrived in Springfield on May 3 to a sorrowful town, prepared to give its fallen martyr a proper, dignified burial. Mary was not in attendance, for though she hated the house that had sapped her husband of his strength, she couldn't find the will to leave. Robert was the only Lincoln present at the funeral. The final arrangements themselves were in some turmoil. The city had bought the land adjacent to the Edwards home in the city and had begun to build the tomb there, but Mary would not permit it. In the final weeks of his life, Abraham had told Mary to bury him in "some quiet place." She wanted him interred at Oak Ridge Cemetery, out of the center of town, but city officials carried on with their plan, ignoring her orders. Only when Mary threatened to bury him in Chicago did they finally relent.

Thousands descended on the small town, the largest gathering in Springfield up to that time. In the state capitol building that Lincoln had moved there himself, his neighbors and friends said goodbye. Then an elegant hearse gifted by the people of St. Louis took the coffin through the streets of the city, past the places he knew in life. At Oak Ridge, he was placed in a receiving vault until a suitable mausoleum could be built and was eulogized for the final time by the Reverend A.C. Hubbard. And so, under the gaze of so many who knew him in life and those who had not, the story of Abraham Lincoln came to an end.

BIBLIOGRAPHY

Abraham Lincoln Bicentennial Foundation. "William Wallace 'Willie' Lincoln." 2019. http://www.lincolnbicentennial.org/resources/abraham-lincolns-life/lincolns-family/william-wallace-willie-lincoln.

Andreas, A.T. *History of Chicago*. Vol. 1. Chicago: A.T. Andreas, 1884.

Baringer, William E. *Lincoln Day by Day: A Chronology 1809–1865*. Vol. 1. Edited by Earl Schenck Miers. Dayton, OH: Morningside House, 1991.

Barton, William. *The Influence of Chicago upon Abraham Lincoln*. Chicago: University of Chicago Press, 1923.

Blatter. Lecture, meeting of the Lawndale-Crawford Historical Association, Chicago.

Burlingame, Michael. *Abraham Lincoln: A Life*. Baltimore, MD: Johns Hopkins University Press, 2008.

———, ed. *At Lincoln's Side: John Hay's Civil War Correspondence and Selected Writings*. Carbondale: Southern Illinois University Press, 2000.

Chicago Tribune. "Cheer Up." October 11, 1871.

Donald, David Herbert. *Lincoln*. New York: Simon and Schuster, 1995.

———. *"We Are Lincoln Men": Abraham Lincoln and Friends*. New York: Simon and Schuster, 2003.

Drury, John. *Old Chicago Houses*. New York: Bonanza Books, 1941.

Dunne, Edward. "Marquette and Joliet Discover the Mississippi," in vol. 1 of *Illinois: The Heart of the Nation*. Chicago: Lewis, 1933, 26–35.

Elliff, John T. "Views of the Wigwam Convention: Letters from the Son of Lincoln's 1856 Candidate." *Journal of the Abraham Lincoln Association* 31, no. 2 (2010): 1–11. http://www.jstor.org/stable/25701816.

Emerson, Jason. *Giant in the Shadows: The Life of Robert T. Lincoln*. Carbondale: Southern Illinois University, 2012.

Fehrenbacher, Don E. "The Judd-Wentworth Feud." *Journal of the Illinois State Historical Society (1908–1984)* 45, no. 3 (1952): 197–211. http://www.jstor.org/stable/40189219.

Flinn, John. *Chicago: The Marvelous City of the West*. Chicago: Flinn and Sheppard, 1891.

Gantt, Marlene. "Abraham Lincoln, Rail Splitter to Well-Paid Railroad Lawyer." *Dispatch-Argus*, February 8, 2013. https://qconline.com/editorials/abe-lincoln-rail-splitter-to-well-paid-railroad-lawyer/article_86e67981-2112-54dd-a4db-bb15ee1aa8a9.html.

Gernon, Blaine Brooks. "Chicago and Abraham Lincoln." *Journal of the Illinois State Historical Society (1908–1984)* 27, no. 3 (1934): 243–84. http://www.jstor.org/stable/40187840.

Goodwin, Doris Kearns. *Team of Rivals*. New York: Simon and Schuster, 2006.

Gourley, James. "James Gourley (William H. Herndon Interview)." Library of Congress: Herndon-Weik Collection. Manuscript Division. Library of Congress. Washington, D.C. 3880–87; Huntington Library: LN2408, 2:124–30. https://digital.lib.niu.edu/islandora/object/niu-lincoln%3A36240.

Gregory, Terry. Chicagology. 2003. https://chicagology.com/.

Grossman, James R., Ann D. Keating and Janice L. Reiff, eds. *The Encyclopedia of Chicago*. Chicago: University of Chicago Press, 2004.

Grosvenor, Edwin S. *The Best of American Heritage: Lincoln*. Rockville, MD: American Heritage, 2016.

Hall, William M., John Wentworth, Samuel Smith, Horace Greeley and Thurlow Weed. *Chicago River-and-Harbor Convention: An Account of Its Origin and Proceedings*. Chicago: Fergus Printing, 1882.

Herndon, William H., and Jesse W. Weik. *Herndon's Life of Lincoln*. New York: Da Capo Press, 1942.

———. *Herndon's Lincoln*. Springfield, IL: Herndon's Lincoln, 1921.

Hill, Nancy. "The Transformation of the Lincoln Tomb." *Journal of the Abraham Lincoln Association* 27, no. 1 (2006): 39–56. http://hdl.handle.net/2027/spo.2629860.0027.105.

Holzer, Harold. *Lincoln President-Elect*. New York: Simon and Schuster, 2009.

Howard, Robert P. *Illinois: A History of the Prairie State*. Grand Rapids, MI: William B. Eerdman's, 1972.

Illinois Gazette. "Speech at Chicago, Illinois." October 14, 1848. https://quod.lib.umich.edu/cgi/t/text/text-idx?c=lincoln;rgn=div1;view=text;idno=lincoln2;node=lincoln2%3A7.

Karamanski, Theodore J. "Civil War." In *Encyclopedia of Chicago*. Chicago: Chicago Historical Society, 2005.

Kasler, Jordan. "Norman B. Judd." Wigwam Warriors. 2014. https://kaslerjordan.wixsite.com/wigwam-warriors/norman-b-judd.

King, William L. *Lincoln's Manager, David Davis*. Boston: Harvard University Press, 1960.

Kunhardt, Dorothy Meserve, and Phillip B. Kunhardt Jr. *Twenty Days*. New York: Castle Books, 1965.

Kunhardt, Philip B., III, Peter W. Kunhardt and Peter Kunhardt Jr. *Looking for Lincoln*. New York: Alfred A. Knopf, 2008.

Lachman, Charles. *The Last Lincolns: The Rise and Fall of a Great American Family*. New York: Sterling, 2008.

Lange, Pamela. *Lincoln's Visit to Princeton*. Princeton, IL: Bureau County Historical Society, 2009.

Laws of the State of Illinois, Passed by the Ninth General Assembly, at Their First Session […] Vandalia: J.Y. Sawyer, 1835. https://archive.org/details/lawsofstateofill183435illi/mode/2up.

The Lehrman Institute. "The Politicians: Norman B. Judd (1815–1878)." Mr. Lincoln & Friends. 2019. http://www.mrlincolnandfriends.org/the-politicians/norman-judd/.

Lincoln, Abraham. *Abraham Lincoln: His Words and His World*. Fort Atkinson, WI: Home Library, 1976.

———. *The Collected Works of Abraham Lincoln*. 8 vols. Edited by Roy P. Basler. New Brunswick, NJ: Rutgers University Press, 1953.

———. Report of Speech to Northwestern River and Harbor Convention, Chicago, Illinois, July 6, 1847. In *Papers of Abraham Lincoln Project*. https://papersofabrahamlincoln.org/documents/D237751.

Markens, Isaac. "Lincoln and the Jews." *American Jewish Historical Society Journal (1893–1961)* 17 (1909): 109.

Mary Todd Lincoln House. "A House Divided: The Lincolns' Confederate Relatives." 2007. https://www.mtlhouse.org.

McIlvaine, Mabel. *Reminiscences of Chicago during the Forties and Fifties*. Chicago: Lakeside Press, 1913.

Meriam, Arthur L. "Final Interment of President Abraham Lincoln's Remains at the Lincoln Monument in Oak Ridge Cemetery, Springfield, Illinois." *Journal of the Illinois State Historical Society (1908–1984)* 23, no. 1 (1930): 171–74.

National Park Service. "Lincoln's Visit to Richmond." Last updated February 1, 2018. https://www.nps.gov/rich/learn/historyculture/lincvisit.htm.

———. "Mr. Lincoln's First Senate Bid." National Park Service History Electronic Library. Accessed December 11, 2018. http://npshistory.com/brochures/liho/first-senate-bid.pdf.

Ostendorf, Lloyd. *Abraham Lincoln: The Boy, the Man*. Springfield, IL: Hamann, 1962.

Page, Elwin L. *Lincoln in New Hampshire*. Boston: Houghton Mifflin, 1929.

Pratt, Harry E. *Personal Finances of Abraham Lincoln*. Chicago: Lakeside Press, 1943. https://quod.lib.umich.edu/l/lincoln2/5250244.0001.001/1:17.1?rgn=div2;view=fulltext.

Pullman History Site. "George Mortimer Pullman." 2017. http://www.pullman-museum.org/theMan/.

Quaife, Milo Milton, and Mabel McIlvaine. *Chicago, a History and Forecast*. Chicago: Chicago Association of Commerce.

Rietveld, Ronald D. "The Lincoln White House Community." *Journal of the Abraham Lincoln Association* 20, no. 2 (1999): 17–48.

Sandburg, Carl. *Abraham Lincoln: The Prairie Years*. New York: Harcourt, Brace & World, 1926.

———. *Abraham Lincoln: The Prairie Years and the War Years One-Volume Edition*. New York: Harcourt, Brace, 1939.

Sautter, Craig, and Edward Burke. *Inside the Wigwam: Chicago Presidential Conventions 1860–1996*. Chicago: Wild Onion Books, 1996.

Simpson, Brooks D. "The River Queen Conference: March 27–28, 1865." *Crossroads* (blog). https://cwcrossroads.wordpress.com/2015/03/27/the-river-queen-conference-march-27-28-1865/.

Townsend, William H. *Lincoln and His Wife's Home Town*. Indianapolis, IN: Bobbs-Merrill, 1929.

Tye, Larry. *Rising from the Rails*. New York: Picador, 2004.

Volk, Leonard W. "The Lincoln Life-Mask and How It Was Made." *Journal of the Illinois State Historical Society (1908–1984)* 8, no. 2 (1915): 238–59. www.jstor.org/stable/40194303.

Wendt, Lloyd. *Chicago Tribune: Rise of a Great American Newspaper*. Chicago: Rand McNally, 1979.

Wheeler, Joe. *Abraham Lincoln, a Man of Faith and Courage*. New York: Howard Books, 2008.

Whitney, Henry C. *Lincoln the Citizen*. New York: Current Literature, 2007.

Winkler, H. Donald. *The Women in Lincoln's Life*. Nashville, TN: Rutledge Hill Press, 2001.

Wood, Kevin. "Lincoln's Eulogy on President Taylor: An Example to Others, Lincoln Himself Included." Abraham Lincoln by Kevin Wood. July 25, 2017. http://www.mrlincoln.com/blog/?p=454.

ABOUT THE AUTHORS

John Toman is a historian who served as president for the Lawndale-Crawford Historical Society. His work in historical preservation in western Illinois has saved many old buildings in the area. He lives in Chicago.

Michael Frutig is a writer of both fiction and nonfiction. He graduated from the University of Iowa. He lives in Chicago.

Visit us at
www.historypress.com